Chinese Kara-Ho Kempo

Chinese Kara-Ho Kempo

VOLUME TWO

SECRETS of KI and INTERNAL POWER

Sam Kuoha,
with Ka'imi Kuoha

UNIQUE PUBLICATIONS
Burbank, California

Disclaimer

Please note that the author and publisher of this book are NOT RESPONSIBLE in any manner whatsoever for any injury that may result from practicing the techniques and/or following the instructions given within. Since the physical activities described herein may be too strenuous in nature for some readers to engage in safely, it is essential that a physician be consulted prior to training.

First published in 2000 by Unique Publications.

Library of Congress Catalog Number: 2001 131323

ISBN: 0-86568-201-1

Unique Publications
4201 Vanowen Place
Burbank, CA 91505
(800) 332–3330

First edition

05 04 03 02 01 00 99 98 97 1 3 5 7 9 10 8 6 4 2

Printed in the United States of America

Contents

Preface vii
Acknowledgements ix

Part I: Ki Principles

1. Introduction to Ki Principles 3
   - Definition of Ki 4
   - My Training in Ki 8
2. Principles and Rules 15
   - First Principle: Keeping One Point 15
   - Second Principle: Relax Completely 24
   - Third Principle: Weight Underside 30
   - Fourth Principle: Extension of Ki 34

Part II: Training in Ki

3. Breathing Exercises 45
4. Portrayal of Ki 57
5. Working Within Ourselves 59
   - Controlling Emotions 59
   - Stories of Ki 61
   - Leading Ki 65
6. Breaking Through the Power of Ki 79
   - Accomplishing this Feat 83
   - Breaking with Ki 90

Part III: Massaging with Ki Principles

7. Rhyme and Reason 97
8. Shiatsu 99
   - A History of Shiatsu 100
   - Lomi-Lomi 121
   - Kiatsu 122
   - Oriental Massage 124
   - The Chakras 125
9. Yoga 127

Preface

Unification of Mind-Body

This book presents to readers the inner foundations of Chinese Kara-Ho Kempo Karate. Through my years of training, I have acknowledged many great martial arts masters and teachers. Although many have pointed me in an external direction, I never lost my interest in learning how to use the mind to cultivate internal powers. At first I thought I was only receiving bits and pieces of the puzzle, but I later realized that my training laid a very strong foundation.

In searching for a way to train and teach a student the internal arts, I found several facets to improve my mind-body-spirit attributes. For example, learning Yoga will help teach you the ancient ways of meditation and stretching. It also provides a good balance for learning the correct way of breathing. Training in Yoga has helped me think better and become more relaxed. It has also taught me that by focusing on certain areas of my body, oxygen will enter more freely. Another favorite of mine is Hatha Yoga, whose roots can be traced to 2,000 B.C. This exercise will be explained in more detail in a later chapter.

Ki Principles training has helped calm my mind and relax my body. I also have been able to accomplish feats I once thought impossible. This training stresses the basic fundamentals of staying on your center and controlling your body and mind at all times.

I still have a great deal to learn, but at the same time I have gained a very positive response from those students of my own I have trained. Though some label it "boring," the practice of Ki will establish the center of all things. It will help you understand the meaning of unity, of correct breathing, of positive thinking, of controlling your emotions, and of keeping your mind and body in harmony.

I find so much peace in training with Yoga and Ki. The process of researching and writing this book has helped me approach life with a different prospective. It also has helped me understand serenity and calmness of mind and body. All my time and energy have been dedicated to passing on this great gift. It is my hope that people hear it, accept it, practice it, learn it, and teach others so we can continue growing through positive reinforcement.

It is my wish that in your own applications, you practice and obtain those things, which will help you achieve your goals in life. In our Yoga class we repeat the traditional Hindu Greeting or reverent salutation, "Namaste" or "The light within the body of my soul bows to the light in the body of your soul."

—Grandmaster Kuoha

Acknowledgements

I would like to thank those who made this book possible. First, all those who had a great part in the teaching and training, including, Sensei Charles Kuheana, for allowing me to see and feel the energy as it is extended; Professor William Kwai Sun Chow, for helping me realize that there should be a balance in one's own life and through this balance brings positive Ki which can touch all those around you; Shihan John Damian, for assistance in helping me realize that Ki or Chi can be developed to heights unknown. Also, that through the constant practicing of Ki Principles, one can bring a powerful unity of mind and body; my Yoga teachers, Lanita Varshell and Master Teacher, Brahmacharini Damara Shanmugan, for all their knowledge and insights which have helped me understand the true meaning of peace. Their teachings have inspired me to discover the true purpose of meditation and relaxation. I have discovered an unbelievable way of bringing the body back to its form with free-flowing energy at its purest. This is the concept of life and health, where the balance of these things should and will venture for one's self-being.

Many thanks to those who have taken time out of their busy schedule to help with the illustrations and explanations for this book: Shihan Ben Kahananui, Sensei Ka'imi Kuoha, Sensei Dana Kuoha, Sensei Khoa Le, Sensei Dave Holliday, and Sensei John DeWitt.

Following is a brief history of the people who will be guiding you through this Kara-Ho Kempo book.

Shihan Benjamin Kahananui, Grandmaster Sam Kuoha's most-senior student. He is a veteran of more than 30 years in the martial arts. His rank of Go-Dan (5th-degree black belt) makes him one of the two top-ranked instructors in the Chinese Kara-Ho Kempo Karate System. For the past 18 years he has studied extensively in the internal arts, with a specific emphasis on Shiatsu and Kiatsu under Shiatsu Master, Sensei Steve Sugai of Hawaii. He has also studied the art of aligning the body, making sure all seven chakras are in sync.

Grandmaster Sam Alama Kuoha, promoted to Kyu-Dan (9th-degree black belt) in 1984 by Professor William Kwai Sun Chow of Hawaii. The certificate was also signed and notarized by Professor Chow. Grandmaster Kuoha was promoted to Ju-Dan (10th-degree black belt) by Professor Chow's advisor, Dr. Ronald Perry, M.D., and accepted by Patsy Chow, widow of Professor Chow in 1987. This was done through the direction of Professor Chow while he was alive. All certificates are signed and notarized. Grandmaster Kuoha had been a student in the Kara-Ho System for over 20 years, first from 1958–69 with Professor Chow's student/instructor, Sensei Charles Kuheana. He also studied with Professor Chow from 1977 until his death in 1987. Grandmaster Kuoha has also trained in various other arts, including Aikido, Shotokan, Tae Kwon Do, Hsin Hsing Yee Ti Kung Fu, Combat Tai Chi Chuan, Judo and many weapons training. Grandmaster Kuoha has spent more than 50 years in the martial arts. Although proficient in many art forms, he only claims a degree in the Chinese Kara-Ho Kempo Karate System.

Sensei John DeWitt, a Ni-Dan (2nd-degree black belt) in the Chinese Kara-Ho Kempo Karate System. Sensei DeWitt started in Cody, Wyoming, under Sensei Robert Shepard (national representative) and moved to San Diego to attend law school. A 10-year karate veteran, Sensei DeWitt now trains under and alongside Grandmaster Kuoha. He is a member of the National Advisory Board for the Chinese Kara-Ho Kempo Karate System. He also practices Hatha Yoga, Aikido, and Escrima.

Sensei Dave Holliday started in the Chinese Kara-Ho Kempo Karate System over five years ago as a senior citizen. After retiring from the construction business and moving to San Diego, California, he decided to look for something that would make him stronger and feel better. He discovered Kara-Ho and trained first with Sensei Dave Caruthers and now with Sensei Ka'imi Kuoha and Grandmaster Kuoha. He received his advanced brown (brown/black belt) and trains a minimum of five days a week, twice with Sensei Ka'imi Kuoha and Sensei Khoa Le and privately with Grandmaster Kuoha and sometimes Sensei John DeWitt. He recently broke the brick-breaking record by shattering 14, two-inch concrete bricks with his elbow. He also is involved in Yoga.

Sensei Khoa Le, a Sho-Dan (1st-degree black belt) has been involved in Kara-Ho for nine years. He began with Shihan Chris Mendoza, then Sensei Dave Caruthers and now Sensei Ka'imi Kuoha. A graduate with a master's degree in the health field from San Diego State University (SDSU), he assists Sensei Ka'imi in teaching at her Tierrasanta School in San Diego, Calif., and attends instructor's classes with Grandmaster Kuoha.

Sensei Ka'imipono Renaye Kwai Sun Kuoha, a Ni-Dan (2nd-degree black belt), has been groomed to take over the Chinese Kara-Ho Kempo Karate system, as relayed by Professor William Chow in 1987, just five weeks before his death. She has been training since she was a year old and her martial arts experience far outweighs her time on this planet. She is a member of SAG (Screen Actors Guild). She held a karate national championship for five years running and owns three successful martial arts studios. A graduate of high school at age 12, Ka'imi was crowned Miss Teen Alpine 1998. Other honors include appearing on the cover of *Inside Kung-Fu* in 1999. Besides Kara-Ho she has been involved with Aikido, Arnis, and Gung-fu under Sifu Dwight Love.

Part I

Ki Principles

Chapter 1

Introduction to Ki Principles

Ki has been taught for many years by many instructors, yet most lacked the knowledge and understanding to teach the why, how, and when encompassing this mystical power.

"Think past the object!" "Relax before striking." "Stay focused!" Common commands. Common Ki Principles. Easy to say, yet difficult to teach. If teachers understood the meaning behind Ki Principles, they would have a better chance of explaining it to their students.

Realistically, Ki Principles can be taught in a relatively short time. But there's a big difference between learning how do it and how to apply it to your life. It takes many years—five-to-10 is the average—to develop inner strength. The sooner you begin the better chance you have of mastering its life powers. The practice of Ki will enhance your outlook on life in general and keep you more focused.

A great master once said, "Anyone can move a mountain. All it takes is work." The first step is the hardest. But what a journey it will be.

To a new student the reality of wanting to train may first stem from his desire to learn the physical side of martial arts. It is hoped, however, that he soon realizes the arts are more than kicking and punching, blocking and striking. Hidden beneath the surface is an internal world, which offers the student a lifetime of discovery.

On a recent trip to my homeland in Hawaii, I visited a Zen Temple located in the deep valleys where I used to live and train. As a couple of my instructors and I listened to the administrator's interpretation of the true meaning of Zen, we were engulfed by a warm and positive energy. We understood the feeling of being "in-tune" with one's own mind, spirit, and body. When you start a journey of learning, you should begin with renewed energy, vigor, and enthusiasm. Every day should be regarded as a new experience. As long as you believe every day brings new experiences, then there should be no regrets. This is extension of Ki.

Practicing Ki Principles helps forge the spirit, mind, soul, and body into one's sphere. To be a better person today than you were yesterday, to be a better human being tomorrow than you were today is a philosophy that everyone should follow. This is the philosophy that incorporates the power of good Ki into your life.

Training in Ki Principles will highlight any physical art you choose and will elevate your overall understanding and skill to levels you never thought possible. This practice enhances your training.

Ki is divided into four principles judged by mind or body rules. All four principles are only effective if they are practiced simultaneously. Breaking down each individual principle helps the student better understand how each segment fits into his daily life. Be mindful that this training can help magnify your power many times over; the power of the mind is limitless.

Definition of Ki

How can we define Ki? Does it have what we consider the five basic sense elements, namely: touch, taste, smell, sight, and hear? Koichi Tohei Sensei refers to Ki as "being with the universe." If you can concentrate on a certain object, how much stronger will you be if the thought goes beyond the physical?

In life, people talk about certain hang-ups that keep them from growing. Ki is power, power that we can obtain from the

Deep Concentration

Sensei Khoa and Sensei Ka'imi face each other, concentrating deeply past each other in a horse stance. Inhale through the nose and exhale through the mouth. Concentrate on a point and remain completely still, allowing your mind to remain calm and focused.

universe. Ki can be considered the power that unifies energy and animate objects. Without that binding of energy into matter nothing would exist. Since everything we see has matter, then it's safe to assume everything around us has some type of energy or Ki. It's like pumping life into an inanimate object.

Ki (or Chi as it is known in Chinese) is associated with any type of movement—wind, the ocean, oxygen, the mind in thought, blood, and even exercises. All things must have Ki to exist and more Ki to move.

The three treasures of the Orient are referred to as Jing, Shen, and Ki. Jing is considered the organism, which stimulates the process involved in going from birth to death. It is the source of growth in a living substance. Shen, on the other hand, is the energy behind the power to think and discriminate, to rationalize and reflect. Ki is the ability to bind and animate, give activation and movement. Ki is used more than Shen or Jing because everything around us has various amounts of Ki.

This explanation, taken from a magazine, might help your understanding:

> *"A slightly built woman returned home one day and searched for her husband. She noticed his auto was parked partially in the garage but tilted slightly to the side. She called out several times, but got no answer. Getting a bit nervous she called her neighbor who said that he had spoken to him, but that was nearly an hour ago and he was working under his automobile. She walked to the front of the auto and then saw a puddle of blood coming from under the car. She ran and noticed that the jack, which was supposed to hold up the front end, was bent and collapsed. The front of the car now rested on the chest of her husband, who looked pale and had blood coming out from his mouth and nose. She tried to get him to speak, but to no avail. She thought the worst and tried to get the jack*

> *to work again, but that also failed. In desperation she attempted to move the vehicle by rocking the front. She thought she saw some movement in his legs. Feeling the need for urgency and realizing that if she didn't do something to help he would be lost, she braced herself up alongside the front end of the bumper, got a good grip on it and started to tug and scream. Still nothing, but the screams had attracted the attention of her neighbor. She braced herself again. This time she knew it might be her last chance. With a mighty effort she lifted with all her being and actually picked up the vehicle off her husband just enough so the neighbor could drag him to safety. A 130-pound woman lifts a 2,000-pound vehicle. In doing so she saves her husband's life."*

Could this really happen? This woman summoned all her energy—Ki, if you will—at this moment of crisis and lifted the car. It was at this moment her mind-body concentration was at its most unified state. How different is this analogy to what sometimes happens in our daily lives when an experience leads us to a unification of mind and body? What about the small animal who defeats a much larger foe just to protect her babies?

Moreover, if it is true that law enforcement officers acquire a sixth sense, why can't someone who trains and practices Ki be equally intuitive? That sixth sense is actually one and the same.

Through continuous training in Ki, you not only can develop the same powers, but have them ready at a moment's notice. But it takes time and it takes diligent, prolonged practice. It's not like riding a bicycle; you can't pick it up and put it down like a book. Like everything else worthwhile in life, you get out of Ki training what you put into it. Unfortunately, many start but only few finish. Ki is the essence of living a good and productive life, of practicing and using these principles daily to make your life more positive.

My Training in Ki

When I was but a child of four, my uncle, Joe Mack Makahilahila, used to watch over me. Joe Mack would throw a canvas tarp over the front of the carport and train me in the arts. Being very little, all I wanted to do was play, but he insisted on teaching me concentration techniques.

"Stand there and look at the Puka in the wall," he would shout, insisting I assume a martial arts pose and stare at a spot in the wall. After what seemed like hours (but it was probably more like minutes), he would come in and teach me stances, punches, and kicks. While this was happening, he would have me stand or sit in a position and concentrate on something. If I moved I got hit. The thought of being hit, of enduring pain helped me remain still even as a young child. Looking back, I realize this was my first official training in Ki or Chi.

I trained in Judo at the Palama Settlement when I was young, but being very small, it was certainly a task for me to remain on my feet. One day after practicing Judo, I observed a Karate class being held in a different hall. I watched for a while and considered joining because it looked more like my speed. I asked my mom if I could try this art but she refused my request. In those days we were taught that we had to finish everything we started. I began training in the martial arts because of my slight stature; my build resembled my mother's, who was Chinese, rather than my father's, a pure Hawaiian.

Much later in life, my mother told me she wanted me to become skilled in martial arts so I could beat my father, who had been very abusive to her as well as us children. This explains why she kept my training secret to even my brothers and sisters until she divorced my father.

When I was 12 my mother introduced me to Sensei Charles Kuheana, who was actually my father's second cousin. (It is to be noted that most Hawaiians are related somehow.) It was through Sensei Kuheana that a system called Chinese

Kempo of Kara-Ho Karate was taught. His home was a shrine and was treated with the utmost respect. There were six of us besides Sensei who dedicated ourselves to this type of training. Extensive training consisted of sitting in *seiza* (seated Zen) and concentrating on breathing for nearly an hour at a time.

"Breathe through the nose, exhale through the mouth," was our credo. Part of our ritual was to fully concentrate on a spot in front of us. If we were doing it right, a fly could land on our nose or buzz into our eye and we would not blink or move. Ki was never mentioned during these training sessions; at the time it was merely referred to as deep concentration. I marveled at the way that we could concentrate so deeply during our physical workouts, how you almost knew what the other person was going to do before he did it.

The training went on for hours each day, with much of the time being spent on deep concentration. This aspect of the training separated the physical art from the mental art. In one of the training exercises, Sensei had us stand with our hands straight out to the side and focus on a spot or object with our eyes. He would place two small paper cups on each outstretched hand. To keep the very light-weighted paper cups from falling, you had to remain motionless. Sensei would walk in front of you and without warning, rapidly strike your face just so slightly several times. The strikes were so swift you had trouble counting the number of times you'd been touched. If you flinched, the cups would fall.

This was his way of teaching deep concentration. Many years later during a seminar in my home, he performed the same exercise for some of my students. One of the pupils was my wife, Dana, who is an instructor in the Kara-Ho System. His speed remained intact, but what was more impressive was that my wife never flinched or blinked an eye. Both paper cups stood firm and unwavering in her hands and after it was over, Sensei said my wife's Ki was very strong. He never expected her to stay so focused.

Sensei John stands in a T-stance or high horse holding two small (3-to-6 oz.) paper cups in his hands. He concentrates on a point and stays focused yet relaxed. Breathe deeply yet smoothly, trying to keep the cups from moving.

Grandmaster Kuoha raises his hands across Sensei John's face just inches from his eyes to break his concentration and try to upset the cups. Sensei John, however, maintains his focus and keeps the cups motionless.

One would think that type of training would be sufficient. However, in the years to come other great masters would have a greater influence on my Ki development. Professor Chow's Ki training was far from boring. If Ki is the universe and the strength of unity between both mind and body, I surely learned from the right person. In our training, Professor would always tell me to think farther than I can see. At the time I had trouble grasping the concept, but out of respect I tried.

Because the techniques of Kara-Ho are rapid and have a variety of combinations, they are executed from within six inches of the body's vital areas. The body cannot generate enough physical force to effectively cause damage from only such a short distance, so I practiced thinking farther than I could see. After many years of training and thinking farther than I could see, I was finally able to produce effective strikes from just an inch of my designated vital areas. Professor Chow taught me to have control over my breathing while performing my techniques. And some of the breathing exercises contained in this book are what he taught me to do before training.

I remember Professor and I going over to the local meat-packer's market where he would assist in the butchering of the large hogs (over 200 pounds) by hitting them with vital strikes. In fact, many observers said his way was more humane than the traditional methods. Time after time he would allow the pigs to run by him and using just the slight movement—almost unseen by the human eye—they would flip over from his touch and be dead in a matter of seconds.

After a lot of homework in the area of a direct striking, including how to strike and the essence of thinking farther then I could see, I was allowed to do the same at the local meat-packer's market.

But it was not until I met John Damian while I was working as a law enforcement officer in San Diego, California, that I realized the scope of what I had been taught all these years. Damian is a student of Aikido and heads the Imua Ki Aikido Association headquartered in Florida. His reputation in the law enforcement community is impeccable, having designed the "speed cuffing" method used in many law enforcement communities. A student under Hirata Sensei (Hawaii) and Tohei Sensei (Japan), he is proficient in teaching Ki Principles. Training with Shihan Damian has helped me understand what Ki is and how it works. He also taught me the techniques behind teaching Ki and how to relate it to an understanding of the mind and body. Plus, he taught me how to lead Ki, which allows you to accomplish your task with the touch of a finger.

I have used this knowledge to teach Ki Principles around the world in classes and at seminars.

Chapter 2

Principles and Rules

First Principle: Keeping One Point

This principle allows the mind to concentrate on what you are doing. This principle involves centering the body for balance and allowing the mind to concentrate on one point.

To keep one point you must remember that for Ki to travel through your body, the mind, body, and breathing must be relaxed. In keeping one point the most important factor is learning to relax your mind. If your mind relaxes, you will be able to allow the Ki to flow and control the other principles.

One of the hardest things to do while training in one point is to erase and control your "thinking habits." In a state of calmness, one tends to think about other things—work, chores, travel, or even what you need to do after your training. You must relinquish all thoughts until after training. At first, try to concentrate your thinking to just one subject, such as breathing.

It is important to find your breath, then learn to use your nose and mouth in conjunction. In your Ki training the first step is to find a quiet place. Then sit down or lay in a corpse position and concentrate on breathing. Inhale and exhale as shown in this book. Allow your mind to go into a state of calmness. With a calm mind, you can learn to control breathing as well as your body.

This one point is located approximately two inches below the navel. This is considered your center of gravity and slightly below the halfway mark in terms of body weight. Everything with matter has its weight sitting below the halfway mark.

To practice this first principle, stand with your eyes focused on a spot against the wall. Your back is held straight, your shoulders down in a relaxed state, and your arms at your side. With your fingers tap approximately two inches below your navel. Tap several times until you can feel the sensation of tapping. Stop abruptly and place your hands back at your sides. Think continuously of that feeling. If you have a partner, have him place a hand on your shoulder and push slightly down and backward. If you have obtained keeping one point, your partner should have difficulty moving you. Have him recheck. At the same time make your body rigid and have him push you again. This time you should be easily toppled over.

Another partner training method is to kneel on both knees in a *seiza* position. Maintain a stable posture. Knees should be approximately two fists or slightly farther apart. Sit with the right big toe crossed over the left big toe. Keep your spine erect and extended. Relax the body and mind, but stay alert. Now tap with one hand approximately two inches below your navel several times until you grasp the feeling in your mind.

Quickly place your hands on both knees, thinking only of the feeling you received when you were tapping. Have your partner assume a similar but perpendicular position to you.

Now have him put his hand in front of your knees and push backward. If you are keeping one point, you should become an immovable object and no matter how hard he pushes, you will remain still. Then have your partner tap your forehead and repeat the process. The changing of your focal point should create a much easier target to push.

Sensei Khoa kneels in seiza position and taps approximately two inches below his navel to keep "one point." Concentration on that spot should be recognized and focused. Stay relaxed and keep the mind calm during this exercise.

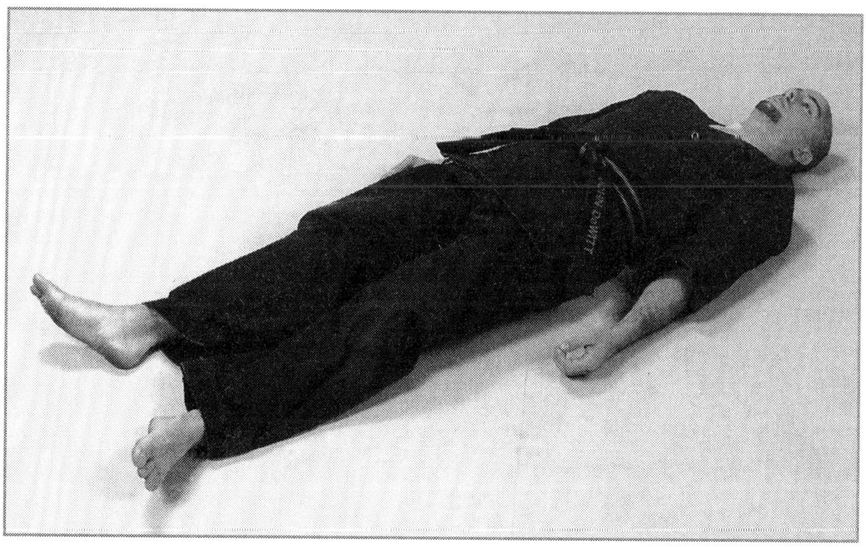

Sensei John lies on the floor in a "corpse pose." He breathes deeply and allows the stomach to rise with inhalation and fall with exhalation. The lower back reaches closer to the ground. Inhale four counts through the nose, hold for four counts, and exhale eight counts through the mouth. Repeat several times. Make a complete circle by lightly touching your index finger to your thumb. Concentrate on calm, controlled breathing.

"One point." Shihan Kahananui taps approximately two inches below his navel. Feet are placed about a shoulder-and-a-half-width apart. The body remains in a relaxed state. He focuses on that one point, remembering what it felt like when he tapped the area.

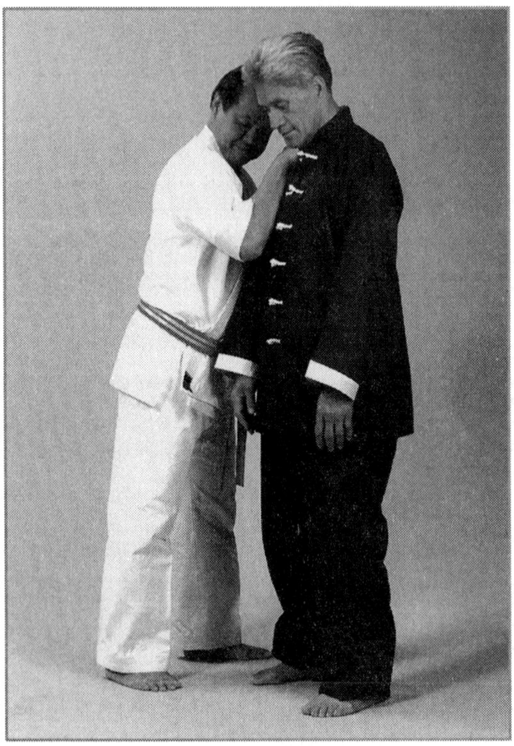

Grandmaster Kuoha pushes the shoulder to force Shihan Kahananui back and down. Shihan Kahananui stands firm.

Grandmaster Kuoha has two men (Sensei John and Sensei Khoa) try to lift him after he practices one point. In this state, your arms hang loose, your feet are planted, and your shoulders are down. Relax and focus on your one point.

Sensei John and Sensei Khoa attempt to lift Grandmaster Kuoha after he assumes the position shown in the previous picture. But they can't budge him. The power of Ki helps the mind control your movements. With Ki training you can easily control your emotions.

Sensei Ka'imi concentrates on her one point and stands stable, with Sensei Dave looking on. She focuses, keeps her body relaxed, and allows her mind to remain calm. Sensei Dave is unable to lift Sensei Ka'imi because she is keeping her one point. In this exercise, the lifter must try the movement without causing any outside distractions, such as squeezing her sides or pulling her forward. The idea is to help your partner become stronger until he or she has sufficient internal power to withstand any outside influence.

Now kneel in seiza position and take another deep breath, allowing all the air and energy to form in the lower half of your body. Have your partner place his hands on your knees and push backward. If you have allowed your body to accept all the energy to the lower half of your body, your partner's attempt to push you backward will be futile.

All your partner has to do to break your concentration is tap you on your forehead. This will cause your energy to rise. When this occurs, you become movable. This time when your partner pushes you, your body will topple backward.

Second Principle: Relax Completely

This is a body rule. The teaching of this principle will be a physical challenge because you will be using the whole body. Because people sometimes have a hard time understanding how to relax their bodies, the understanding between "relax" and so-called "dead Ki" is often confused.

Recent medical research has discovered that people become sick not necessarily from a disease itself, but from stress. When we are stressed we tend to allow our emotions to produce bad or negative Ki, which becomes stagnant. When Ki does not flow, our bodies are more susceptible to attack from within.

We must learn to control our emotions and our appetites with our minds. There are many things in our lives which will produce an adverse affect if we can't mentally control them. They are commonly called the seven emotions and the six appetites. The seven emotions include danger, fear, fright, joy, sadness, pensiveness, and grief. The six appetites are money, fame, sex, wealth, gain, and thoughts of loss. Understanding these emotions and appetites constitute large pieces of the puzzle, but equally important is learning how to control and disperse them once they enter your mind. Ki Principles training will help you control your mind and eliminate these distractions from your daily lives. Trying to control all 13 thoughts would be next to impossible, but through Ki Principles training we can make sure they do not become dominant forces in our minds.

Thoughts come to you in a variety of ways; there's not much we can do to stop them. Where we have power, however, is in how long we allow them to effect us. One way to counteract these feelings is to use the one point or your breathing to elicit another thought into your mind. Although these emotions may force a change in your breathing or cause you to lose one point, concentration as taught in the previous chapter will help you to regain control of your mind.

For example, when you are driving and someone is creating traffic problems or making an unsafe lane change, the first reaction is to get angry. Rather than take it out on the rest of the world, concentrate on your one point, take deep breaths and exhale slowly.

When you get angry, your breathing becomes more rapid and short and your blood pressure rises. A way to counteract the reaction is to quickly start breathing and keep one point. You will notice that your breathing will return to normal and your mind will become calm. The anger disappears as quickly as it came.

To train your body to relax, lay in the corpse position and allow your feet to fall sideways. Your hands are at your sides. Find your breathing and concentrate on your one point. First think of your feet: tighten them and then release. Next, tense the calves, then the thighs. Tighten every muscle below the waist, including the gluteus maximus. Hold this pose for 15-to-30 seconds, then release. Next start on the upper torso. Begin with the hands, then the arms, and finally the body. Tighten, hold, release, then let go. Since the shoulders, face, and back are constantly carrying large amounts of stress, we perform the exercises separately. Tighten the face, lips, teeth, jaw, shoulders, and back, hold for the 15-to-30 second count and then release and relax. You will notice your body feels totally relaxed.

The testing of this principle will be the same as testing for the first principle. There are several ways to practice this and gain the same results.

Other ways to practice this include: Shaking your hands at the wrists so violently that it forces your heels to bounce off the ground. Do this for a couple of minutes, then stop abruptly, take in a deep breath, and let it out. Have your partner squat in front of you, place his hands under your arms and try to lift you. Or you can have him place his hand on your shoulder and try to push you backward. Tapping the forehead slightly will break his concentration and disturb his one point.

Another method is to have the person run in place as fast as he can for a short time and then tell him to abruptly stop. Now repeat the training exercise. He can also go down on his knees and follow the example in the first exercise.

Relax completely. Sensei Khoa Le shakes his hands so hard his heels bounce off the floor. He does this for about 30 seconds. Partner Sensei John DeWitt has control over the situation and when he feels Sensei Khoa has created a strong physical energy base, he will tell him to stop. After Sensei Khoa stops he takes a deep breath. He should feel the energy traveling all the way to his feet. Sensei John should not be able to move or lift Sensei Khoa. This is another example of keeping the one point, except instead of funneling energy through the mind you are using the body.

Another way to push energy through the body is to run in place, lifting your knees high and quickly pumping your arms and hands. When Sensei John feels the physical energy has reached its height, he will tell Sensei Khoa to stop and take a deep breath.

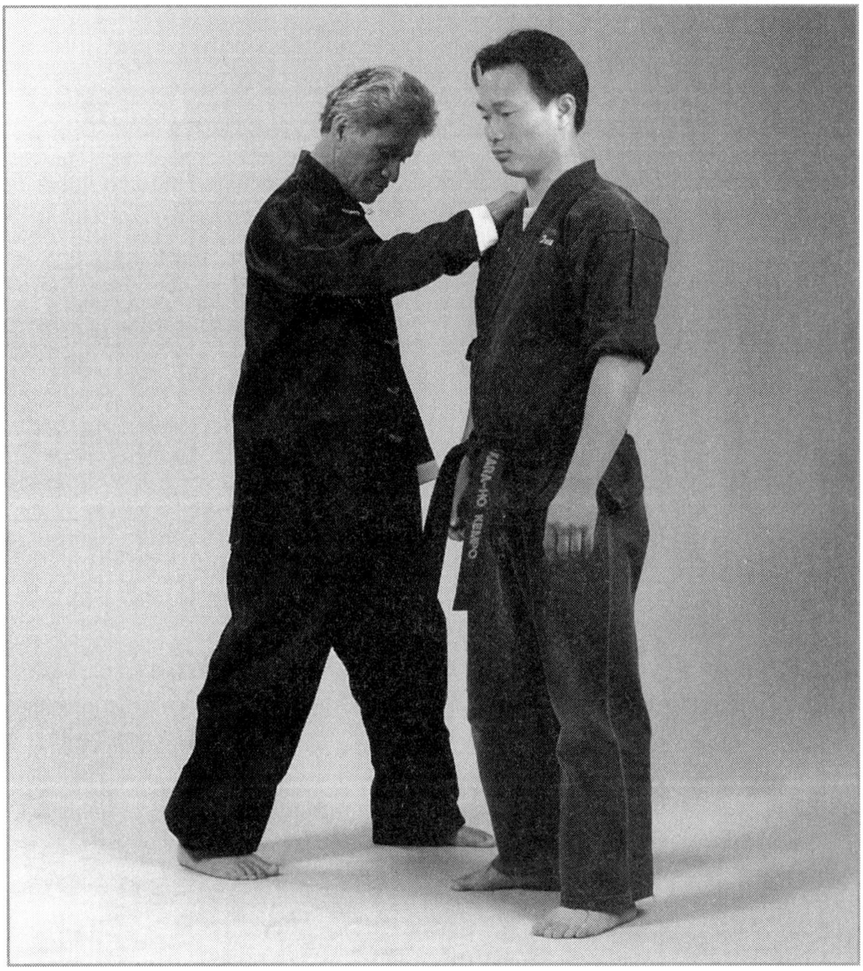

After Sensei Khoa runs in place or shakes so hard his body gets physically worked up, he stops and relaxes with deep breath. Sensei Khoa assumes an upright stance, knees a shoulder-width apart. Shihan Kahananui tries to push him back, but his efforts are futile.

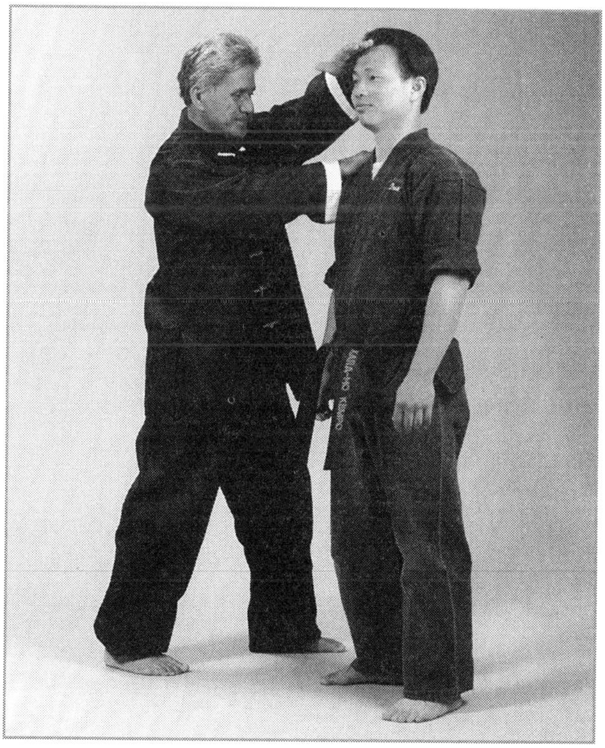

However, by tapping Sensei Khoa's forehead, Shihan Kahananui breaks his balance. Sensei Khoa's balance moves from his one point to his forehead.

As shown here, Sensei Khoa topples backward. After much training and practice, Sensei Khoa eventually will be able to stay strong and focused even when someone taps him on the forehead.

Third Principle: Weight Underside

This is also a body rule. While one of the hardest rules to understand, it can be very effective in the performance of your techniques. Keep in mind that even if you have not been effective with the principles, you must be doing them all. One only works in harmony with the others.

If you relax completely, the weight of your body will naturally settle on the bottom or underside. If we keep one point (#1), we can relax. If we relax completely (#2) all the weight will settle on the lowest portion. If the weight settles at the underside (#3) we can remain calm through mind and body.

By gaining more control of your mind, you allow the weight of any portion of your body to be lighter or heavier simply by concentrating on low or high. If you wish to make your arm lighter, just think on the topside; if you want it to become heavier, just think underside. It is said that you can lower and raise your blood pressure in an instant simply by allowing your mind to think of an emotion that will raise or lower your heart beat. For anger, it will rise. For sadness, it will be sporadic. And for lower, just concentrate on your breathing and your body and mind will flow into a state of calmness.

To experiment, get a blood pressure machine and take your reading at a normal pace. Remove the machine then concentrate as hard as you can on raising your blood pressure. If you think about something that makes you angry, your pulse rate should speed up. Take your blood pressure again and see if you were able to make it rise. Now concentrate on breathing and slowing your pulse rate by thinking of your one point. After a few minutes, take your blood pressure again. Your heart rate should have slowed.

There are several training methods which will help you practice this exercise. With your partner standing beside you, have him extend his arms straight out, clench a fist and cause his arm and shoulders to become rigid. Clench your fist and stand perpendicular to your partner's arm. Now try to push his arm down with force and strength using your fist. The chances of you succeeding are 50/50. This time, relax your arm and simply drop it directly across your partner's tense arm. Just allow the weight to fall. You should be able to make your partner's arm fall toward the side. Think past your partner's extended arm and concentrate on dropping your own arm directly to the side.

Another example is to partially bend your arm outward. Have your partner raise the hand while it is tense. He should accomplish this with little effort. Then with your arm out practice the first three principles, making sure your mind is calm and your body is relaxed. Now extend your arm again, then have him try to raise the arm. He should find the task much more difficult.

Learning the fundamentals of this principle is difficult, but once mastered it can be effective in your pursuit of any martial art. Just remember: The principles are like the wheels of a car. Four working together make the journey go smoother.

Weight Underside. Sensei Dave makes his arm very strong and defies Sensei John to push his arm down. This is pure strength against pure strength and the strongest will win.

By totally relaxing and allowing the falling arm to absorb all the weight, Sensei Dave's arm will drop from the heaviness.

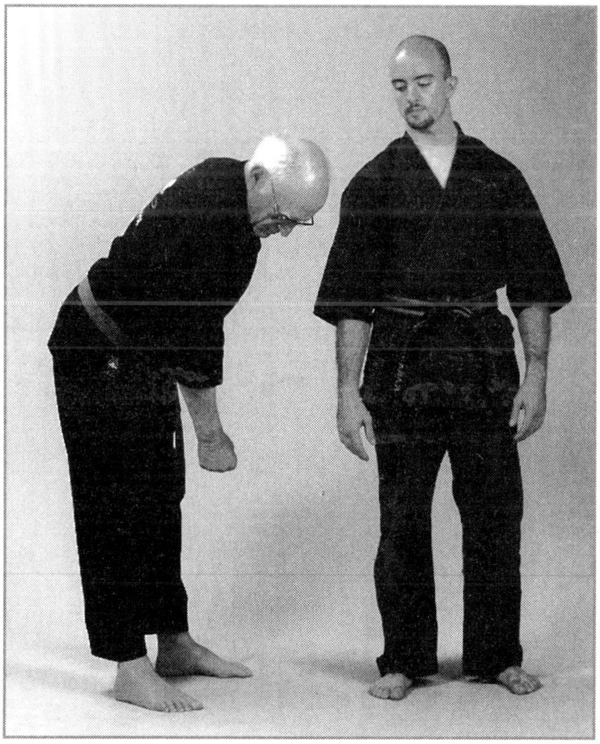

Notice how the body drops when the arm is lowered. When one limb is tense the body follows suit. When you feel anger, the tenseness is transferred to various areas of the body. That's why stress can cause stiffness in the back, neck, and throughout the body. This kind of emotion destroys the center and breaks down the control of your mind.

Grandmaster Kuoha bends his arm at the elbow and allows the weight to sit on the underside of his arm. Sensei John attempts to push up the arm, but is unsuccessful in moving the arm or the body. The arm is at a relaxed state with no force. If force or tension is placed on the bent arm, it will move upward.

Fourth Principle: Extension of Ki

This is a mind rule. Although one of the most utilized terms in any martial art, it also is one of its most misunderstood aspects. The practice of Ki allows your mind and body to become one with the Universe. If you wish to become stronger internally, then you must keep up the training. Several examples follow.

The concept of "unbendable arm" provides the framework for teaching the extension of Ki. The training starts with extending your arm outward as in "weight underside." Place your arm on your partner's shoulders and see if he can bend it at the elbows using both his arms. There should be little trouble accomplishing this task.

Note: Be sure your practice partner is about your size and weight so variables do not come into play.

Next, stretch out your arm, fingers extended, and concentrate on touching a focal point in the distance. Keep your arm relaxed, yet concentrated, extend and reach as if there was a steel bar connecting your fingers to your focus point. Allow your mind to run freely by thinking of a spot much farther than your eyes can see. Have your partner once again try to bend your arm. This time it should be much more difficult.

Many accomplished breakers use this principle quite successfully by thinking through the object(s) they are attempting to smash **(see the chapter on breaking).**

When you have been practicing Ki Principles for a while, you might want to practice another exercise to help the flow of Ki.

Kneel down in a *seiza* position. Have your partner stand facing you. Concentrate on your one point then bow slightly forward at the waist so the tops of your shoulders are equal to your knees. Keep your head up so you can see and extend through your partner's body. Have your partner place his hands on your shoulders, thumb next to the fingers. Take your hands and lightly touch his elbows, fingers extended and elbows down. Now imagine your fingers are going directly up through his body and out through the other side. Keeping his body upright, have your partner push you backward, each time exerting more pressure. Make it a gradual push rather than being a jerky motion. Although the pushing becomes more intense, you should be able to withstand his pressure. Now get up quickly and push him back, extending your energy through him.

Another way to practice is to take your forefinger and thumb and press them together very tightly using every ounce of strength you can muster. Have your partner pry them apart. If you're only imagining that you are stronger than your partner, he should be able to pull apart your thumb and finger. However, if you think that both finger and thumb are merely providing a complete circle that cannot be separated, then you have set your mind on your one point. Therefore, it will become nearly impossible for your partner to pry the digits apart.

Remember: The objective is to help each other become stronger by using Ki. It is not a matter of who is physically stronger, but who can use his mind to become focused and relaxed. That's where true strength enters the picture.

You can also revert power back to your partner. Grandmaster Kuoha kneels in seiza position as Sensei John attempts to push him. Not accepting Sensei John's power, Grandmaster Kuoha instead reverts it back to his partner by softly touching his elbows and concentrating through his body. The result is that Sensei John cannot push Grandmaster backward.

Even with the help of two men, it becomes impossible to move Grandmaster Kuoha as long as he remains relaxed in body and mind.

The "unbendable arm." Sensei Ka'imi extends her arm and concentrates on her fingers reaching out and focusing on a subject away from her. Because her fingers are extended, her arm becomes sturdy like a steel bar. In her mind she is touching something. No matter how big or strong a man is, if her arm is fully extended and her mind is focused, her arm cannot be bent—provided, of course, that all other Ki principles are followed.

This is another way for younger people to exhibit Ki extension. Stand with your feet a shoulder-width apart and concentrate on breathing. A younger person's short attention span makes concentration difficult at first, but practice makes perfect. Grandmaster Kuoha has successfully taught some as young as three years of age. Have the older person squat directly in front of you and then pick him straight up. The older person will be able to pick up his partner with ease. Be careful not to squeeze under his arms or pull him forward.

Next, have the younger person put his index fingers on either side of the larger person's neck as Sensei Ka'imi is doing here with Sensei John. Have him concentrate on making the fingers try to touch each other. I call it "The Frankenstein." Tell the younger person to pretend the fingers are actually bolts and they must travel completely through the neck. Ask him if he can really see it. Tell him he can become Frankenstein if he can make the bolts touch each other. Then have the older person slowly lift him up—and be sure it is straight up. It should be next to impossible to lift the subject, regardless of his slight stature.

The harder Sensei John tries to lift Sensei Ka'imi the easier it is for her to concentrate. This is where internal power becomes more prevalent.

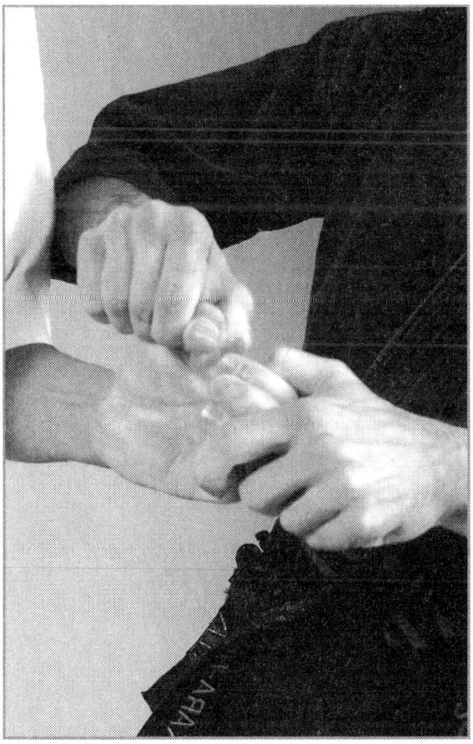

Extension of Ki. Another exercise is to tightly hold your index finger and your thumb together. Now have your partner try to pry them apart. It should only take about 50 percent of his power to do so.

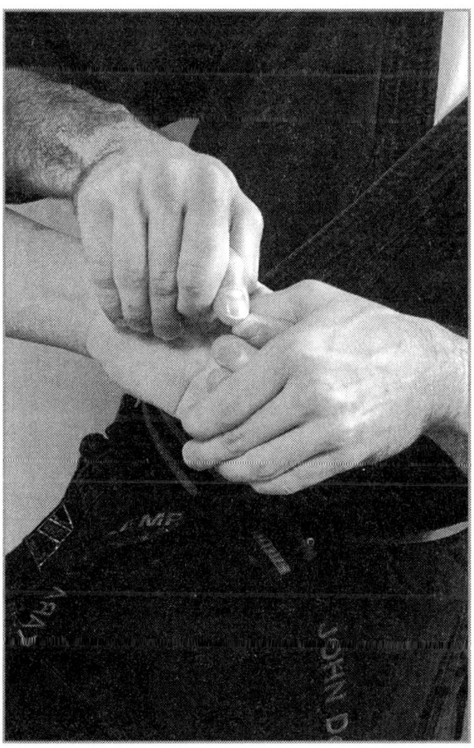

Repeat the opening process, but concentrate on making your thumb and finger into a complete circle. Make sure that no tension exists in that hand. Your partner will find it nearly impossible to pry the digits apart.

Part II

Training in Ki

Chapter 3

Breathing Exercises

The concept of true breathing stems from the diaphragm. True breathing cleanses the mind and body and invigorates the blood flow to all parts of the body. Breathing correctly also helps massage and cleanse the body's vital organs.

One posture that promotes healthy breathing is assumed by lying completely flat on your back. This is called the "corpse" pose. Keep your feet about a foot apart and your hands at your sides. The fingers are apart but the thumb and forefinger are lightly touching. Keep your shoulders down, spine aligned from the Atlas (just below the skull) to the sacrum (lowest triangle bone). Let the arch in your lower back form as the rest of your body lies flat on the ground. Concentrate on your breathing by inhaling through your nose. As the diaphragmatic muscles pull oxygen in, your stomach will rise and deepen the arch in your lower back. Then exhale through your mouth, slowly forcing the air out. Make the exhale at least twice as long as your inhale, allowing your spine to return to normal, vertebra by vertebra.

Shake your body if you find it hard to relax. Start from below your waist and tighten the muscles in your legs, feet, buttocks, and hips. Now concentrate on your breathing. Perform the same movements from the top of your waist. This should help you release some of the tension in your body and allow you to fully venture into your own breathing. Good breathing should start at a 4–4–8 count (that is, breathing in for four counts, holding for four counts, then exhaling for eight counts). Use your diaphragm on the inhale and concentrate on the breath going through the nostrils. Hold the breath deep down in the stomach and then let it out ever so slowly, forcing the air from the stomach by pushing with the diaphragm. The breathing should become rhythmic and slow. Bring in the air around you when you inhale. Try to feel the purity and warmth as it penetrates every part of your body. Keep the concentration at the one point, located just below the navel. It may be hard at first to focus on staying relaxed, but the more you practice, the better you'll become.

As in Yoga, the concentration and breathing become deeper and the positions are extremely relaxing. Those who train in Yoga on a regular basis can actually massage the different meridians in detail and allow the flow of oxygen to be delivered to every part of the body, including the glandular areas.

To practice relax-tension breathing, stand with your feet about a shoulder-and-a-half width apart, feet pointing forward. Bend your knees outward and down to form a "high horse stance" or "T-Stance." Keep your back straight and erect, shoulders back but down, chin tucked back, and hands alongside your body. The fingers are open.

Start with your hands at your sides. Now reach for the sky, extending your arms and hands well above your head. Inhale through the mouth for a count of four. Hold for a four count. Turn the palms outward and exhale through the nose for a count of eight while lowering your hands to the side. As your arms come down past the halfway mark start to clench your fists until they reach your side, then relax. Feel the blood rush through your body as you force all the air out and constrict the diaphragm. Repeat this sequence three times, while concentrating on your one point.

In this next exercise, draw your arms, open hands, and elbows backward. Use a four count, hold for four, then push the hands outward with the palms facing out toward the front with an exhalation of eight count. Repeat this three times.

In this last exercise, draw your arms and hands back over your head for a count of four. Your shoulders are going backward. Hold for four counts when you reach full extension, then extend your hands down and back across the front, palms facing down, for a count of eight.

When doing any other breathing exercises, try doing them with these counts. You may not be able to do the 4-4-8 at first. It is best to start lower and work your way up.

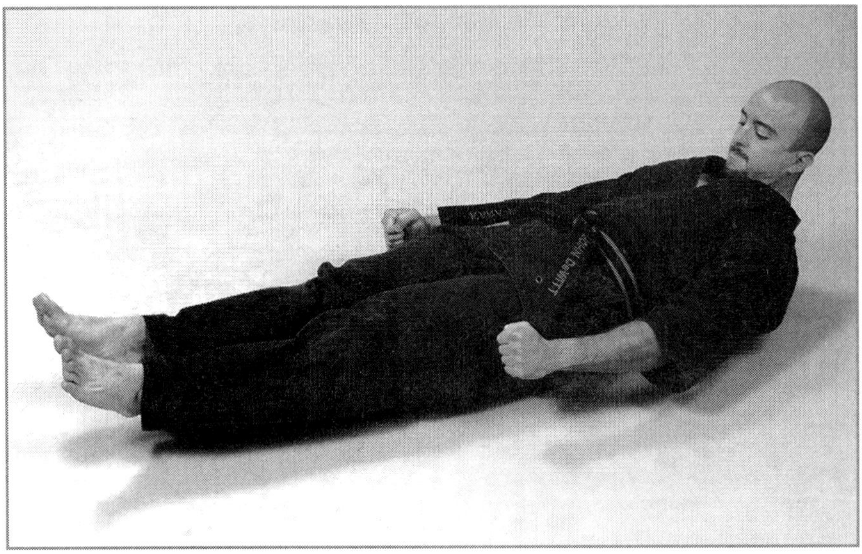

Start from a "corpse pose." Stiffen your body, legs, arms, head, neck, and shoulders. Hold for a few seconds.

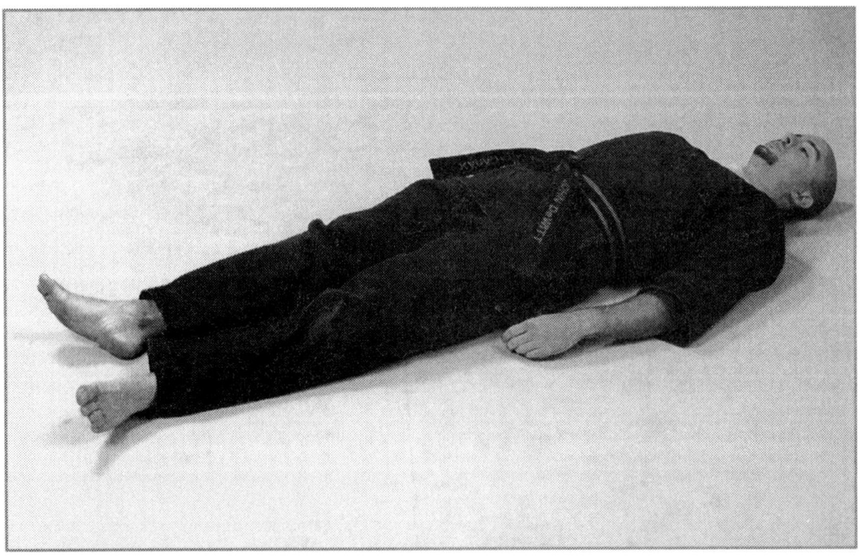

Now let everything go limp. Set your feet about a shoulder-length distance apart, then drop your shoulders and fingers. Now relax the arms.

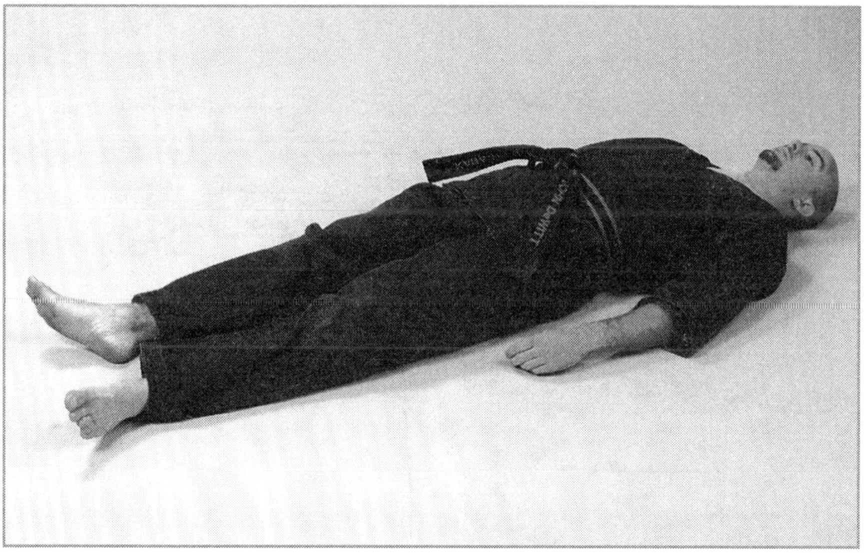

Breathe deeply, allowing your stomach to rise with the inhale and sink with your exhale. Your breaths should be slow and calm, with twice as much time spent on the exhale as on the inhale.

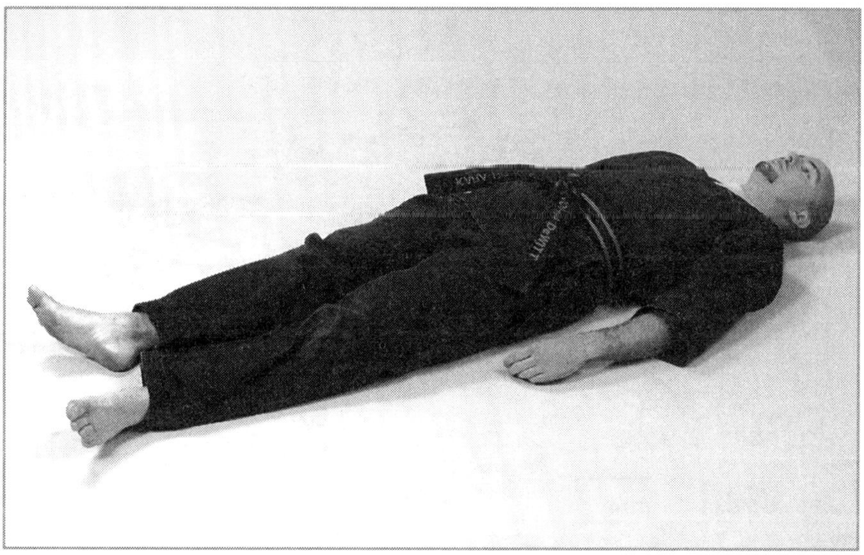

Fall completely into a relaxed state. Concentrate on your breathing, allowing your breath cycle to reach your feet as well as your head.

Stand in a high horse with feet pointed forward and approximately twice your shoulder-width apart. Starting with your hands at your sides, push your hands upward toward the sky, inhaling through the mouth and exhaling through the nose. This is referred to as "reverse breathing." Push your arms all the way up and then exhale, forcing the arms slowly down to your sides.

These breathing exercises are the same as those previously featured except they are performed standing.

Stand in a medium horse stance. Bring your elbows straight back and slowly inhale through your nose. Hold for a few seconds so the oxygen can purify your organs.

Force the air out by pushing your arms straight forward. Make sure you exhale at least twice as long as you inhale.

At the end of your breathing finish with a full extension of your arms.

Chapter 4

Portrayal of Ki

Daily exercises will assist you in becoming stronger as you develop your Ki in centering your one point. It is important in everyday life to portray "good" (positive) Ki as opposed to "bad" (negative) Ki. Have you ever experienced a day where everything goes wrong? You tell yourself, I got off on the wrong side of the bed this morning and now everything has gone bad. It's because you have portrayed this negative Ki from the time you left the house. If you feel that everything is going to go bad, most likely everything will. But if you feel that everything has a purpose and you will enjoy the day, no matter what comes about, you will portray positive Ki. Rather than complaining about rain because you just washed the car, tell yourself pure water from heaven is falling to nourish to flowers. This type of Ki turns the negative feelings into positive images. In other words, the person who just cut you off on the freeway merely was trying to get to his destination a little faster.

If you maintain good, positive Ki everywhere you go, you will naturally center your universe at one point and will receive good results. But if you don't exhibit healthy Ki, the effects will be negative.

Your outlook can also change the way others feel. The power of Ki takes so much focus that those who spend their time in Ki training can bring the universe into their center.

Those are the people who can heal themselves with an aura that effects everyone around them. It is truly the unity of body and mind.

Two elements of the universe make up our lives: the body and the mind. It can be expressed in terms of the body responding through the dictation of our mind and/or the mind expressing itself through the body. They are inseparable and are our form of survival. If they have the full comprehension of motive, we can gain the perfect realm of unity.

Your mind is the center of your responses. If you allow your mind to be weak, then you will be weak. But if it gains strength, you will endure constant growth. Many people allow themselves to get sick by convincing themselves they will. I know a doctor who constantly tells himself he's going to catch a cold every time he comes in contact with someone who has the virus. And sure enough, in a couple of days he has the virus. Why does that happen and how can we eliminate those thoughts?

The training of Ki Principles and different types of Eastern philosophies will help the mind become stronger. Since we know the mind controls the body and its functions, we can exhibit good or bad ki. We can truly say the body moves in accordance to what the mind relates, and the mind symbolizes itself through the body. Both work in unison and cannot be separated.

Chapter 5

Working Within Ourselves

Controlling Emotions

Ki is within everyone and everything created on this Earth. It is the coalition of the universe within ourselves. As human beings, we are rulers and have dominion over everything else; we have the power to reason and the knowledge to grow. Although man has tremendous powers, much of our capacity to learn and understand is never used. Much of this power, referred to as Ki in Japanese and Chi in Chinese, is often misunderstood.

I recently watched a television account of a fighter pilot preparing for battle. As he walked around his jet, he made sure all the missiles and guns were in good working order and that all the instruments functioned properly. He also checked his parachute and as soon as he took flight, he made sure the radar was registering.

As human beings we should make sure that our mind and body are equally united. We must design our lives to avoid accidents, diseases, and even destruction. If it's cold outside, we make sure we're wearing ample clothing. If we are driving, we make sure the vehicle is safe for driving and we have enough gas to get from points A to B. If we do not care about how life is and what hand we are dealt, then we will remain stagnate. But we'll progress if we chose to develop our lives to be more positive.

We were born to prove our worth. Some of us are blessed

with great and helping families and friends. Some are not as lucky. We all have been given control of our minds and the power to "reason." We also have the power to choose right from wrong.

In a recent encounter, a large man who was suffering through a bad day approached one of my students who has been studying Chinese Kara-Ho Kempo Karate for four years. The bully began yelling. My student stood his ground, but chose not to get involved in an argument. Although the bully did everything to pick a fight but throw a punch, my student remained relaxed. The following day found the bully at it again. The bully pushed and prodded. Finally, after failing to draw my student into a confrontation, he struck the first blow. Forced with protecting himself, my student used several restraints to subdue the bully. The police were called and several witnesses vouched for my student. The end result: Kara-Ho student 1, bully 0.

Typically, an instructor who did not teach Ki would have told his student to take care of the situation immediately. In essence, teach the bully a lesson by beating him to a pulp. And had this occurred 25 years ago, I might have exhibited the same reaction. However, those students who have been taught true Ki principles know a unification of the mind and body allows you to control your emotions. As long as you keep one point, as long as you stay focused and calm, you'll be able to handle any situation.

A footnote to the story is how the student came to me four years ago. A weightlifter, boxer, an all-around sports enthusiast, he enjoyed contact sports—especially street fighting! Although he never started a confrontation, he never backed down from a challenge, either. In effect, he never saw a fight he didn't like to join. But on this day with this bully, he proved he had defeated the toughest opponent of all: maintaining a calm presence when many would have lost their cool. He showed he could be a man! I was truly proud of him because he took what I taught him and made it work in his life. Since then, he has become a role model for others to follow and will make a fine instructor for many years to come.

Stories of Ki

As you proceed in your training of Ki, you will start to see some changes in your ability: some dramatic and some subtle. No matter how they unveil themselves, you will undoubtedly feel more calm and your outlook more positive. Many will actually see the change before you do. Your emotions and appetites will be more controlled and you will be able to forgive faster than ever. While some already have these gifts prior to training in Ki Principles, there is always room for improvement. Your senses will start to be more sensitive and you will start to see and feel things more clearly than ever before. Remember the saying, "Slow down and smell the roses?" Practice of Ki will enhance all your senses, allowing you not only to smell the roses, but to enjoy them as well. Joining the rapid pace of the "rat race" can easily disturb your "one point" and clutter the mind. Those who begin training in Ki principles will notice varying degrees of strength. That strength will come and go until you become proficient at maintaining a level of calmness and serenity. The goal is to attempt to feel Ki all the time. When that happens, you can be considered a true master. We owe it to ourselves and those around us to portray good or positive Ki; this, in turn, brings forth good Ki.

You can practice by finding a quiet place. It can be a favorite wooded area, the shores of a lake, or a park. Sit and look beyond your surroundings, hear the sounds, smell and recognize the objects, absorb the environment. Concentrate and meditate on these things for a while. Then lightly close your eyes and see if you can picture those same sounds and smells. A quiet room will do just as well. You will probably hear things you never heard before, see things you never saw before, and smell things you never smelled before. This is sensitivity training—much the same way a law enforcement officer looks beyond his nose for things out of the ordinary or listens for unfamiliar sounds. This is called the sixth sense or Ki.

Working with many fine police officers has shown me that some possess varying degrees of Ki training. In the beginning I was schooled by a superb training officer who showed me that police work was as much feeling as it was reaction. Learning this as a police officer put me into a different frame of mind. When I was at work, my Ki became stronger; but away from work, I noticed a drastic decline in my emotions. Like the woman who lifted a 2,000-pound vehicle off her dying husband when the need arose, I was using my Ki when my mind was open to the experience. Ki is formed and developed when you train in it all the time.

Have you ever walked into a crowded room and sensed that you shouldn't be there? Or have you disliked someone at a first meeting but didn't know why? This is part of your Ki. Remember, people who have bad Ki will portray bad Ki and people who have good Ki portray good Ki.

My Yoga teachers told me the first time they met me and my students they felt a strong aura of peace. This aura is called Ki or internal energy—energy from the universe.

As a police officer I received the nickname of "Dog-Man." Although one of my side businesses is training dogs, I got the moniker because I was involved in a situation where I used my Ki to sense and capture a couple of burglary suspects.

Here's how it went down: I was working the midnight shift in an area of San Diego not known for its peacefulness. I responded to a silent burglar alarm coming from a large department store. My beat partner arrived first and I was a few minutes behind. When I got there my partner said he had checked the premises and determined it was a false alarm. We combed the perimeter and found all doors secured; nothing out of the ordinary. We notified dispatch and went back into service. A short time later we were notified of the same alarm. Again we got there, looked around and saw nothing out of place. On any second notification a building must be checked more thoroughly so the security for the business arrived and opened the doors. By that time five additional officers had arrived so we decided to have a dog unit check the area. Dogs are often used because they can sniff out a problem in much less time. The canine unit, which has a very strong sense of Ki, was unleashed on the building. After 30 minutes, the dogs and their handlers came out empty-handed. We returned to service. Five minutes later the alarm sounded again. This time the dispatch notified two canine units and myself. This time a different handler and canine entered, but the result was the same. A short time later the same alarm went off and we were obligated to conduct a thorough search. The manager of the store and a police supervisor joined local store security. The security guard arrived first along with my beat partner and myself, and so we decided to search the inside.

I entered the building with my partner, while the guard stayed outside to notify other officers not to enter while we were in there. We walked to each department at the store, chatting normally as we went along. I suddenly had a feeling we were not alone. Now mind you, there was nothing tangible on which to base this feeling. It was like someone was staring at me from across the room. I stopped, relaxed, and focused on the feeling. I realized that someone was hiding in the ceiling ducts above our heads.

When I quietly mentioned this to my partner, he burst out laughing and told me I was crazy. I again pointed to the ceiling and picked up a long rod from one of the clothes racks nearby. I thumped on the ceiling, identified ourselves and racked a shell into my shotgun. A frantic voice rang out from the ceiling saying: "Please don't shoot. I'm coming down!"

My partner jumped back as if he had seen a ghost. The suspect jumped down and we calmly placed him into custody. He told us he was working alone.

But as we walked him out of the building, we passed a small cabinet-type closet, which was directly in the center of the aisle. I got that same sensation when we passed the cabinet. I stopped in my tracks. My partner looked at me, and shouted, "What? You smell someone else?" I nodded in the affirmative, kicked the bottom of the cabinet and identified myself. A voice from inside the cabinet shouted, "Please don't shoot!" My partner jumped back, throwing down the handcuffed suspect, removed his revolver and stared at me with a bewildered look.

We removed the second suspect and walked both outside to the waiting arms of an audience of officers, a canine unit, store managers, security officers and some bystanders who had been awakened by the constant flashing lights. The supervisor confronted my partner who was senior to me and asked how we found them. He quickly pointed to me and announced that I had a nose better than the canines that were trained for this sort of work. From then on, the name "Dog-Man" stuck. Imagine writing that kind of report and handing to a representative in the District Attorney's office.

"While sniffing the area, I located a pungent odor of another human being besides my partner and me in the area high above the ceiling etc."

Many other things can be controlled through the use of Ki. I was once told after a seminar that what I was teaching appeared to be "Black Magic." People tend to only believe things they can hear, see, or feel. But there is another, more powerful side waiting to be discovered. With the use of Ki you can actually feel through walls and announce what is on the other side. Try opening a car by mentally raising the door lock. Try feeling where a nail holds a piece of wood when the naked eye cannot see. And try moving a ton of roof without moving a muscle. Just Ki. Just unifying the body, mind and spirit.

Leading Ki

To define leading Ki, you must understand the purposes of Ki Principles. If you practice Ki Principles and have developed an inner strength that makes all things around you seem positive, then perhaps many approaches need not be negative or confrontational. However, when push comes to shove there are times when you must defend yourself.

Leading Ki is another way to defend yourself while remaining calm and relaxed. It is an expression of a non-violent approach to defense, a way of getting others to do what you want them to do without physical or verbal contact.

Here is a true story of using "leading" Ki to defend yourself. Several people stood talking in the middle of a large gymnasium. A young girl decided to prove a point so she looked up convincingly toward the ceiling. Although no one said a word, others followed her lead by looking up. More people filed into the gymnasium, each taking their cue from the first lady. This went on for several minutes until the young girl who started it all went outside. However, she proved that without eye contact or saying one word she could get others to do what she wanted them to do. This, I believe, is a trait of leading one's Ki.

When I was in law enforcement, I was often called to the scene of a family dispute. Without saying a word, I often was able to calm the situation merely by my presence. Even though these situations were heated, I approached with a relaxed body and calm mind. Positivity and calm replaced negativity and chaos.

In today's world too many people meet violence with violence and negativity with negativity, because the understanding and practice of calmness is contrary to human nature. We must stand up for our rights, no matter what the cost. Sometimes force is justified, but in a majority of the cases we can stave off violence by handling the situation in a positive manner. How much better would this world be if we didn't have to worry about leaving our doors unlocked or our eyes forever peeled.

In recent studies, we see that if a person views things in a positive light, others will take advantage of him. But I have learned that one should never mistake kindness for weakness! One can safely say that you can lead another's Ki by eye contact, physical movement, verbal interactions, and even thought. Leading one's Ki in combat is to confirm your mastery of this powerful art.

It should be noted that these leading Ki techniques are usually done in less than a 1 1/2 seconds. The techniques are shown because they provide a way for the reader to see how to lead one's Ki as opposed to stopping one's Ki.

1. Leading Ki Attacks. In leading one's Ki, you first must be relaxed when the attacker approaches. If you are tense, leading your opponent's Ki becomes impossible. The object of leading Ki is allowing your opponent a different target as he attacks.

2. As Sensei Khoa attacks Grandmaster Kuoha, Grandmaster pivots away from the attack and moves his hand quickly in front of the eyes of Sensei Khoa. This actually gives the attacker a different focus.

3. After Sensei Khoa's attack goes by, Grandmaster then stops Sensei Khoa's Ki by pushing his palm to his face and nose area. This will force Sensei Khoa to either take the hit to his face, or stop abruptly and risk taking a backward fall.

1. As Sensei Khoa attacks, Grandmaster Kuoha slides backward and uses his right hand across Sensei Khoa's eyes to give him a new focus.

2. Grandmaster drops his hand on top of Sensei Khoa's using weight underside and guides the attacking hand.

3. Leading the hand around in a counterclockwise fashion, Grandmaster Kuoha sets up Sensei Khoa to move in the same direction he wants to go. The purpose of leading Ki is to establish the attacker's movement in the same direction.

4. As Grandmaster Kuoha leads Sensei Khoa all the way around, he finally stops Sensei Khoa's Ki with a hand to the face. Either Sensei Khoa has to take the hit or drop back to the ground. Either result would end the attack.

1. Sensei Khoa bearhugs Sensei Ka'imi from behind and pulls her slightly backward.

2. Reacting quickly, Sensei Ka'imi slides her left foot back slightly into Sensei Khoa, who already is pulling her in that direction.

3. Sensei Ka'imi then extends her right arm forward, bends at the knees and tilts her body to the left to allow Sensei Khoa's momentum to go forward.

4. Sensei Khoa takes the fall as his forward progress cannot be stopped. Leading his Ki means guiding him in the direction he is intent on going.

1. As Sensei John attacks Sensei Ka'imi, she remains calm and relaxed so her mind and body can function in unity.

2. Sensei Ka'imi slides back and gives Sensei John a new target with her hand quickly going across his eyes.

3. She instantly drops her hand on his attacking fist using weight underside. This forces his arm to drop and his body to dip thanks to weight underside.

4. She repels him upward and back by bringing her thumb and hand across his nose and face.

5. Sensei Ka'imi then finally relaxes her hand on the downward motion, slamming Sensei John on his back.

1. Sensei Khoa gets ready to attack Sensei John.

2. As Sensei Khoa attacks with a looping right-hand punch, Sensei John remains calm and relaxed, sliding off to one side and guiding his right hand across Sensei Khoa's eyes.

3. He instantly drops his right hand on the attacking arm and creates a weight underside.

4. As in the section on weight underside, the movement is done in a rapid, straight-down motion.

5. The motion of weight underside forces Sensei Khoa to lose balance. When his arm is forced to the ground, his head and body naturally follow.

6. Sensei Khoa either takes a dive face first or makes the roll.

Chapter 6

Breaking Through the Power of Ki

This chapter explains how through internal energy I was able to perform various breaking feats. This power eventually landed me on the cover of "Breaking Power" (*Inside Karate* magazine's largest-selling breaking issue ever), led to performances all over the word, and gave me exposure on several national television shows, including "The Tonight Show with Jay Leno."

I was taught at a young age that developing breaking power was 80-percent mental and 20-percent physical. You cannot perform breaking techniques overnight. Like any great skill, planning and preparation are your keys to success. If you are planning to break with your hands, make sure your hands have been well-prepared. That means treating the hands both before and after each session.

At a recent tournament, I watched several contestants from white through black belt hold their hands after their breaks. Some hands were even bleeding. Later, I learned that many had injured their hands through any combination of the following: a lack of physical preparation; a lack of correct technique; or a lack of proper mental attitude. Our students, however, were much more fortunate. They not only managed to overrun the competition, but walked away injury free. In fact, my students tore through the ranks with such ease judges wondered aloud if the breaking materials were altered. Except the tournament sponsors provided the materials!

Even with that realization the judges checked and rechecked the materials for any altered flaws. They found none.

My mentor, Professor William Kwai Sun Chow, once told me if you DO NOT work with the tools of your trade constantly, you will get rusty and be clumsy when you need to use them. This advice came from a man whose tools were as razor sharp as they come, a man who never wasted a motion, a man who could use his skills to clear a room (see photos of his two front knuckles). In the martial arts, we are constantly using our hands, feet, and mind—generally every part of our body. Many martial artists agree that to become proficient in your art it takes several years, but to remain proficient takes a lifetime. One cannot train for five years, stop and come back a year later and expect to be sharp.

Sensei Kuheana (one of Professor Chow's students and one of my instructors) told me that when you think you know everything, you have learned nothing. But when you admit you know nothing, you will learn everything. Years later in his own Hawaiian Pidgin English Professor Chow reiterated the philosophy. To this day, I am still trying to improve; our work in the martial arts is never done, our task never complete.

When training a portion of your body for breaking, be sure you're learning from a qualified instructor. You risk potential permanent injury when you either train without an instructor or receive training from someone with improper knowledge. There are many good training aids on the market today, most of which are markedly improved over what was available to me when I started. There is no substitute for a master who has undergone the experience of learning how to break the right way. Remember to do your homework. The damage that can be done to your bones and muscles over a short period of time could live with you the rest of your life.

This entire book deals with developing personal focus and the practice of Ki Principles. If you set out to seriously practice Ki principles, not only will your techniques become stronger, quicker, and more proficient, but there will be a drastic improvement in your breaking skills. During all my breaks, the objects in front of me are already destroyed in my mind. All I have to do is perform the physical act of breaking. At no time during the entire performance is there a chance of me failing. Granted, there have been a few times when objects were tougher to get through than I expected, but they were nothing I couldn't handle with additional will. This attitude was set in my mind from the first time I decided to do any breaking feat. My Ki was extended and I was always on my "one point."

Professor Chow taught me that a breaker with doubts is like a baseball hitter walking into the batter's box with the count 0-2. Suppose someone tells you there is a 50-50 chance you might be able to perform a certain break. If you go into the break with that attitude, your chances of succeeding will be no greater than 50-50. Breaking is not an endeavor you enter unless you are absolutely sure you can do it. There's no other way to approach it. Anything less than 100-percent certainty is asking for trouble—and the very real chance of sustaining serious injury.

During a recent martial arts television broadcast from Florida, two black belts competed for the "world championship" in breaking. One stylist tried to break 12, two-inch concrete bricks with a ridgehand technique. He exhibited tremendous physical power and his feet lifted from the ground and he crashed hard into the bricks. Unfortunately, only seven bit the dust. Tragically, he also suffered a dislocated shoulder.

The second competitor set up his bricks and with a hammerfist technique, bettered the first competitor's mark by shattering eight bricks. Both men claimed they had over 20 years of martial arts experience. Recently I had one of my students attempt a similar breaking feat. His name is Dave Holliday, a 68-year-old martial artist with a little over five years experience in Kara-Ho Kempo.

David stacked 10 bricks made of the same material and tried the break. Up to that point, he had only attempted to break five bricks. We sat down prior to the performance to determine the state of his mind. As we spoke he asked me specifics about the breaking technique then told me what he hoped to accomplish on his 68th birthday. I told him that he had to imagine the bricks were already broken, that the preparation already was done in his mind. All that was left was the physical act. I added that if he thought his chance of success was 50-50, he was risking serious injury.

After we set the bricks, I confidently whispered to him that these bricks are really nothing more than objects in his way. He approached the bricks with confidence and total relaxation, shattering all 10 bricks with one hit. He moved back and with an astonished look on his face said with pride, "Hey, that wasn't too bad."

Less than a month later, he broke the world record with a mark of 14, two-inch concrete bricks weighing over 322 pounds. He was stunned, because it came so easy he didn't think he had broken all 14. It just goes to show that as your Ki gets stronger, you tend to think less of what you are doing or trying to accomplish. You are becoming so confident in yourself your expressions are defined as casual and the thoughts not nearly as evident. Sensei Dave Holliday is becoming a person who portrays true Ki in everything he does.

You, too, can accomplish the same type of feat. Breaking does not have to be one of your goals. Whether or not your aim is martial arts, the training of Ki Principles will heighten your focus and increase your will to succeed.

Accomplishing This Feat

After you have trained your body to withstand the punishment of breaking, it is now time to decide which materials you'll put to the test. It is a good idea to start with easier objects before you experience the difficulty of harder materials. It is also better to start with one object and work your way up. Many people make the mistake of biting off more than they can chew. And when the attempt fails, they cannot recover from the negativity.

Begin by placing the object on your base, and then placing another item (focus material) on the ground below the subject matter. Stand or kneel next to the subject matter and look at the focus material below. Position your hand or another object on your subject matter, while still looking at the focus material. Do this several times until you have the correct position and can actually visualize the focus material. Relax, tap your "one point," and continue to view everything in front of you. During the break, although you must concentrate on the subject matter be sure to focus on the material below it. If you have practiced Ki Principles correctly and diligently, you will be amazed at your power—not physical, but mental power. Once your have begun your breaking regimen, proceed slowly and carefully.

Breaking Preparation

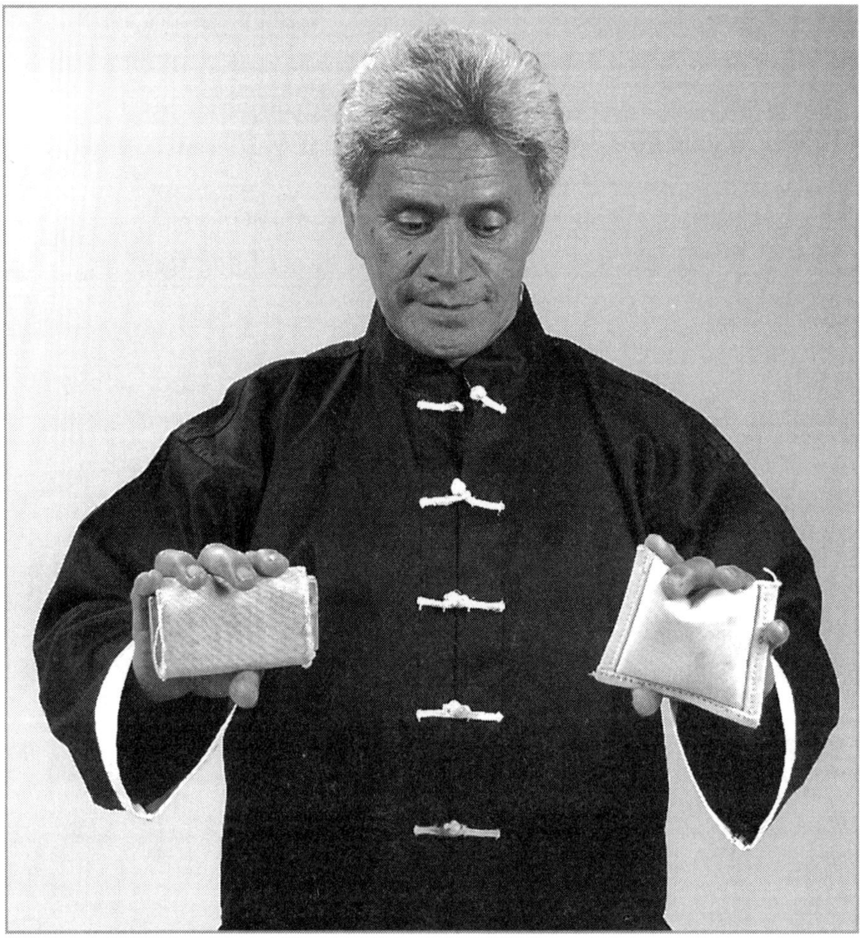

Shihan Kahananui holds some of the portable equipment used to build various parts of the hands and arms. The miniature sandbag is made of heavy canvas, it measures approximately five square inches, is double sewn all the way around, and packed with clean, sterilized sand. It also is small enough to fit in the palm of your hand. The small, custom makiwara board can be made by cutting a piece of half-inch plywood measuring approximately two-and-a-half inches by four inches. Sand the board to eliminate the possibility of splinters, wrap a tightly woven manila cord around the board, then hold it together with wood glue. Now take a heavy canvas piece, which will fit around the cord, wrap it around the makiwara and place a few small tacks at the end to hold in place. Soak the equipment in dai jow for sterilization purposes. These pieces were designed by Grandmaster Kuoha.

Utilizing the Sandbag

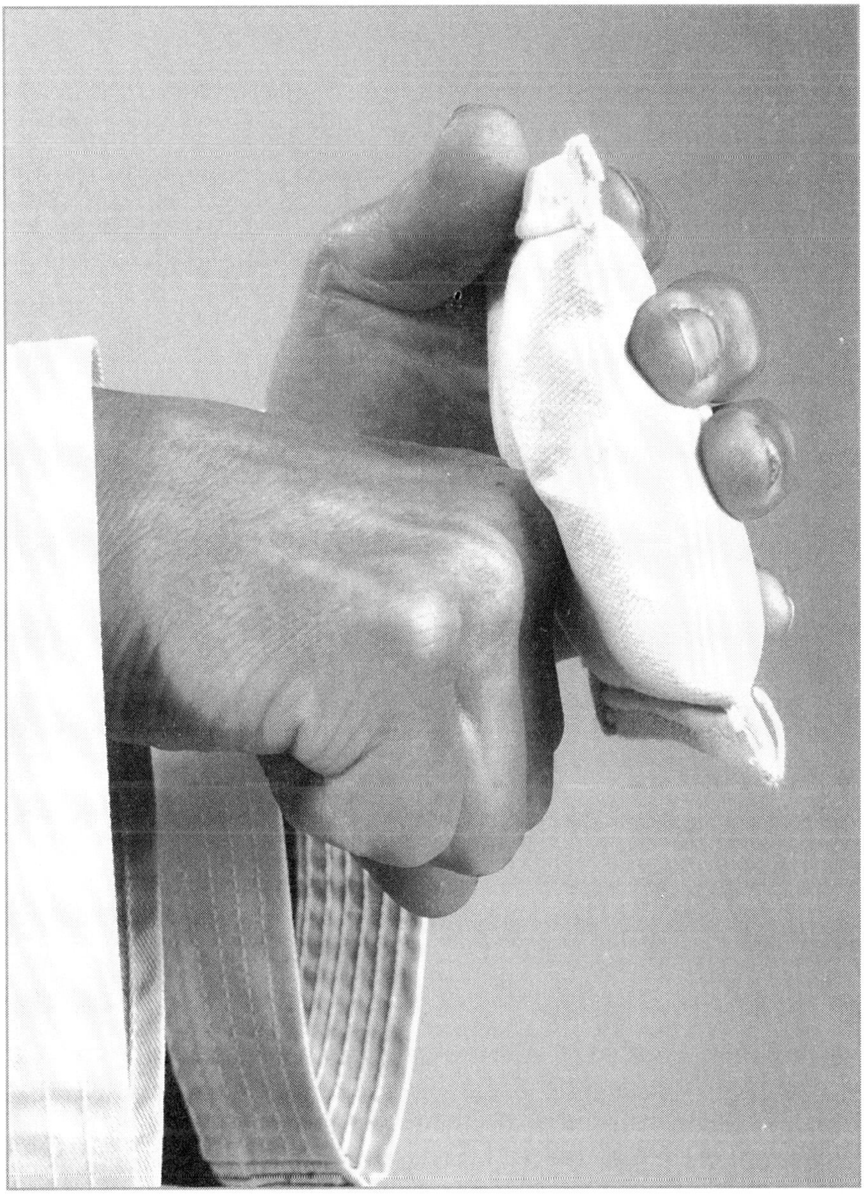

Hold the sandbag in one hand and, using just the two front knuckles, punch the bag with a rolling motion to work the front knuckles. The bag should be used until a callus forms on the knuckles; then go with the board. These were designed small enough to use it anytime, even while in your vehicle.

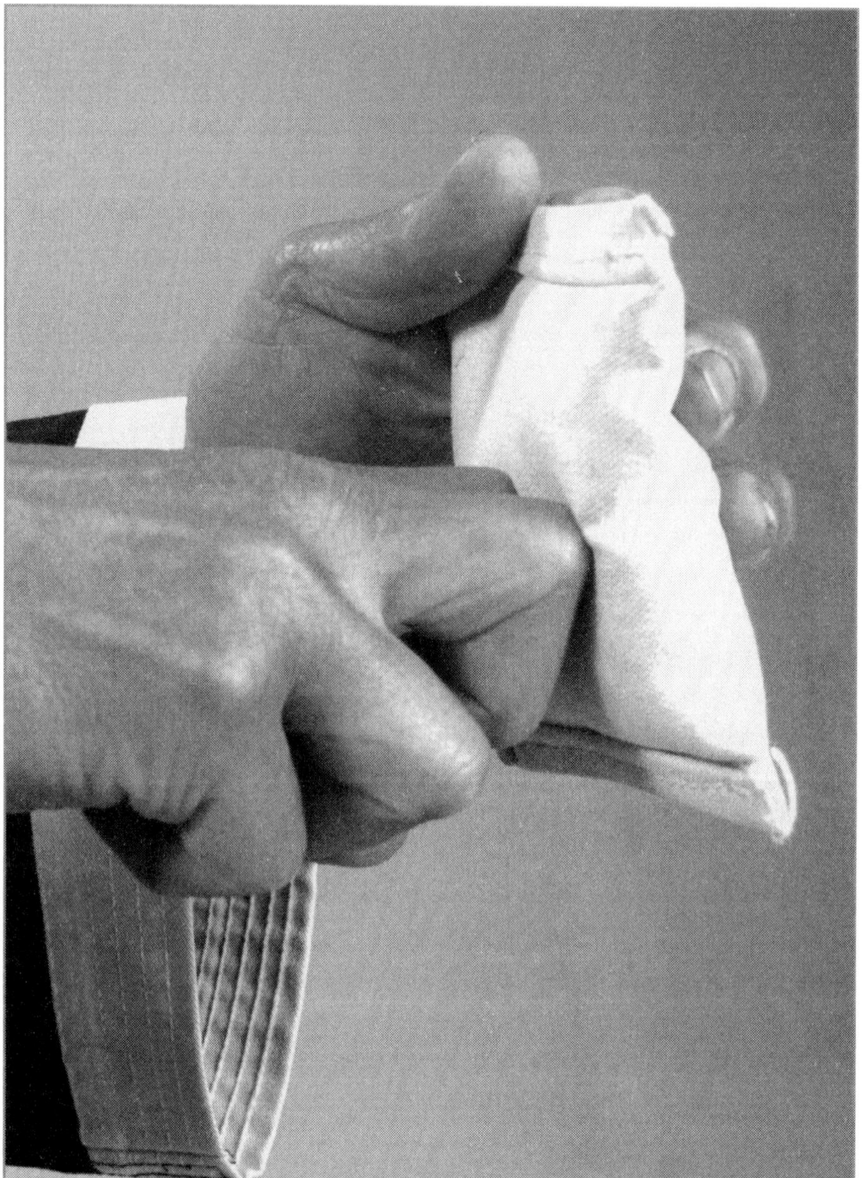

Since using the center knuckles is imperative to mastering Kempo techniques, build up calluses on the sandbag before moving on to the board.

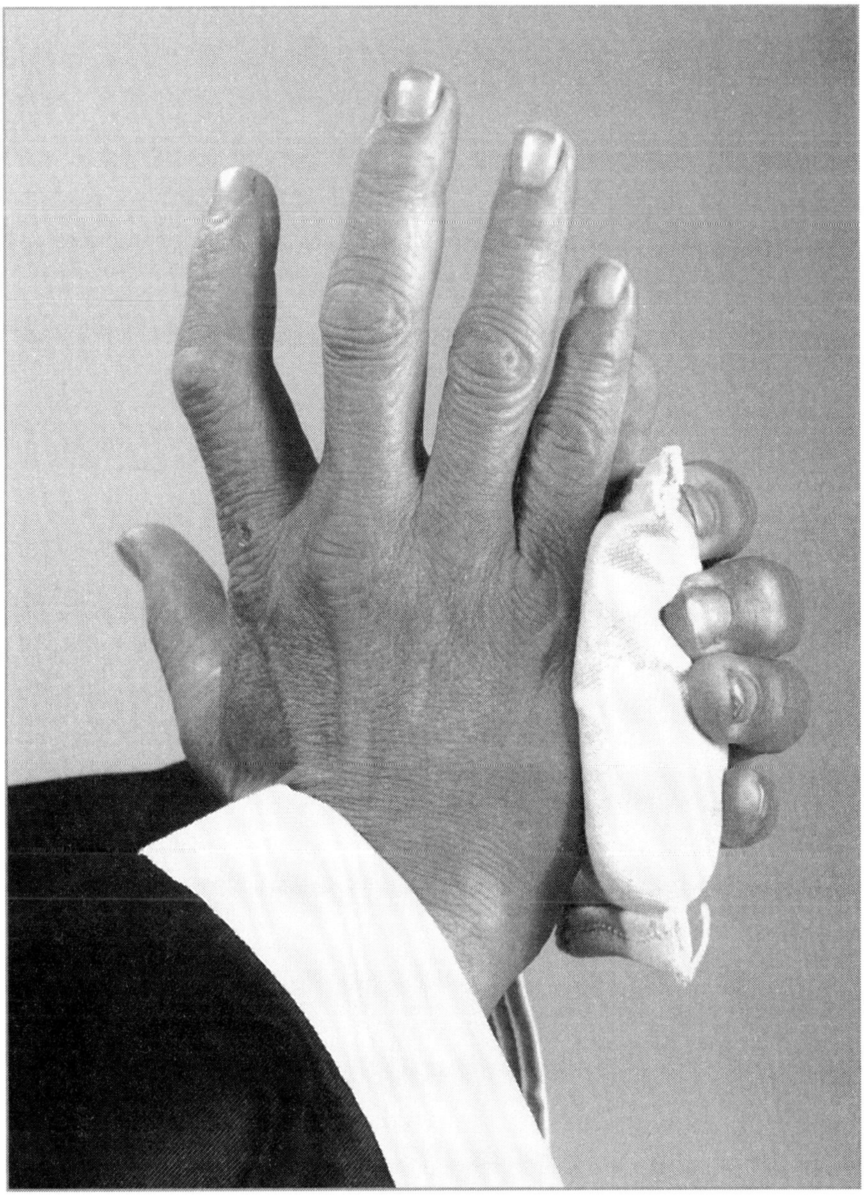

Using the cutting edge of the hands is one of Kempo's favorite tcchniques.

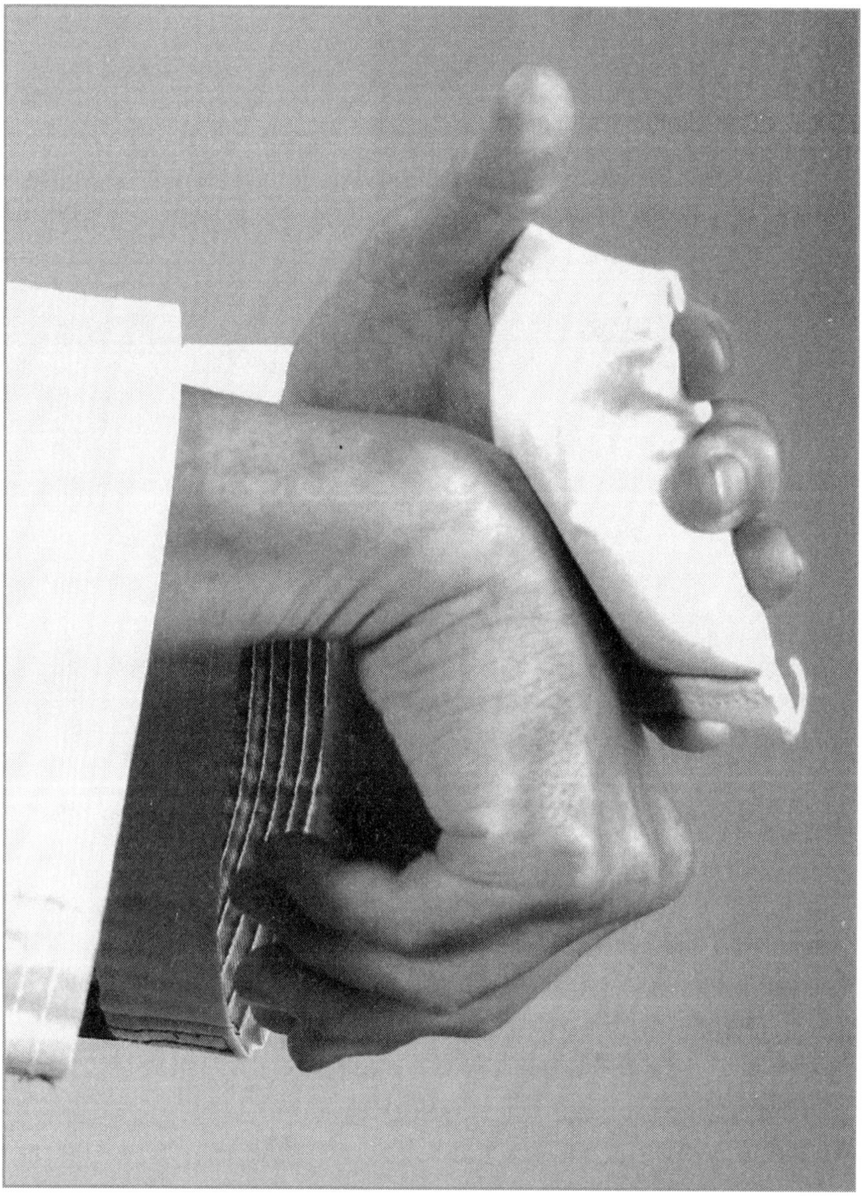

In the art of Kempo, the back of the hand is a favorite striking tool, especially during crane neck techniques. This portion of the hand must be trained and developed.

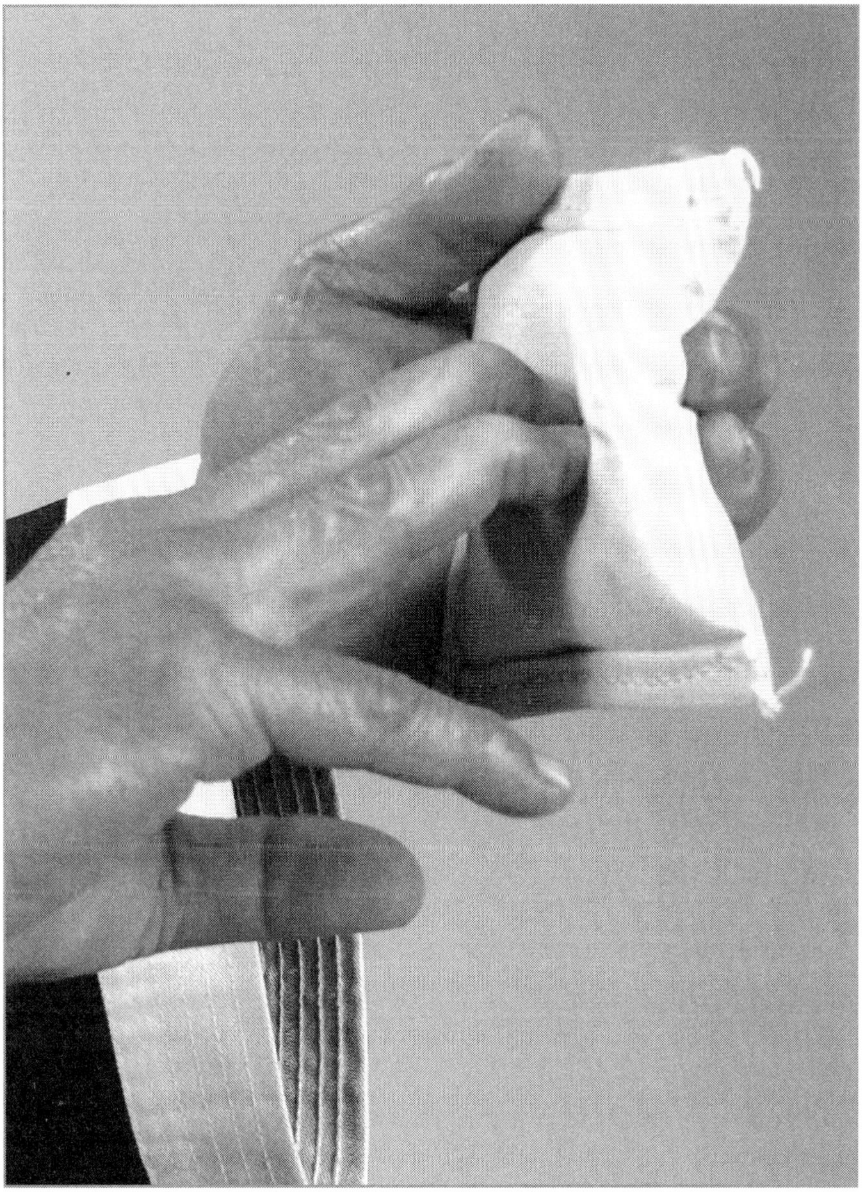

Utilizing the fingers is important. But because the extended fingers are fairly weak, they should be trained and developed. Professor Chow used to work the fingers so much that calluses would form at the very tips of the fingers. Several times he was observed puncturing sandbags with his fingers.

Breaking with Ki

Sensei Dave Holliday demonstrates breaking by using Ki Principles. Utilizing all principles but accentuating on "weight underside," he raises his arm high above his head, relaxes, and then attempts to break two, two-and-a-half inch concrete bricks perched on two drinking glasses.

Sensei Dave focuses on his primary target, making sure he is centered and directly over the object to be hit.

Sensei Dave visualizes on the target resting on the floor. He makes sure his arm is calm and totally relaxed.

As you can see, Sensei Dave's arm is totally relaxed, his concentration is sincere, and his hands are open. As long as you break with Ki, you reduce the chance of injury. You can also achieve much more by breaking using Ki than relying on power alone. Using Ki principles in breaking allows anyone of any size, shape, or age a legitimate chance to achieve his goals. As you can see in this demonstration, the drinking glasses remain intact. If power by itself was used, the glasses in all likelihood would have been shattered.

Part III

Massaging with Ki Principles

Chapter 7

Rhyme and Reason

The practice of massaging will enhance Ki flow. Several methods are used to help in these practices. Shiatsu, acupressure, acupuncture, deep massage, and kiatsu are several of the more popular methods for relaxing the body. Their purpose is to open Ki channels and allow the Ki to flow freely through both the giver and the receiver.

When suffering from trauma a person will naturally open these channels by yelling, shouting, or jumping up and down. This opens the blood flow, which forces Ki through your veins. You may start to rub or massage the injured area, which forces the dissipation of stagnate blood flow. Ki will start to flow in its place. This keeps old blood from forming and allows new blood to enter the injured area.

Before you start to massage, be sure you maintain the fundamentals of Ki Principles, meaning you are relaxed and keeping "one point." It is important that when you are massaging, you focus on the task at hand. If your mind wanders you won't receive full benefit from your actions.

Massage can be used for a variety of reasons. It helps promote the healing process by restoring energy flow, and helps you relax by keeping the mind and body in tune with each other. This serves to release tension.

Utensils used for massaging include the fingers, elbows, palms, and side of hands and feet. Basically, use whatever helps you relax. Whichever method you choose, make sure your mind penetrates through the muscles and bones. If you're working on an injured area, work deep into the sore points and over the injured area. Start off lightly and then work deeper with the massage as long as the mind can take it. It is best to begin the massage with your hands because they are the best conduit of Ki. As you get better with extending Ki you can experiment with other methods. Studies have shown that receiving or giving massages on a daily basis can reduce illness and even disease. The reason is simple: Giving or receiving massage like the kinds in this chapter will increase your awareness and Ki transfer. This heightens your concentration and relaxation of both mind and body.

Chapter 8

Shiatsu

The combination of shiatsu and stretching is important. Shiatsu pumps energy (Ki) in the area by improving the body's circulatory system, helping add flexibility and allowing your muscles to be more relaxed. Your mind will be calmer and your thoughts positive.

Shiatsu therapy strengthens the muscles and reactivates the free flow of energy into the body. It helps to prevent or reduce the effects of illness by stimulating the body's natural cells and allowing its own recuperation through applying pressure to certain points of the body.

Eastern philosophy originally referred to the art of massage as *anma*. It was first sighted in China and then moved to Japan in the 1600s during the Edo Period. Early practitioners saw the curative effects of using the hands to apply serious pressure to injured areas of the body. The 19th century saw *anma* being taken over by Western massage techniques. Though they share the same roots, they differ in many respects. They're application—which featured strong, solid pressure using the hands for rubbing, kneading, stroking, and pounding—produced dynamic results.

The Japanese therapeutic method of massage referred to as shiatsu was in direct contrast to *anma*. It was much calmer in nature and required the soft and fleshy parts of the hands and arms to massage. It was designed to gradually apply enough pressure to reduce soreness and stiffness.

Penetration of the muscle tissues was limited to what

would help blood and energy flow freely. This type of massage would invigorate the muscles and allow the body to heal itself. The modern system of shiatsu determines specific points of the body and devises the most suitable manual techniques for various parts of the body. These points are then pursued through the surface by means of pressure.

Even in modern times, the many variations of shiatsu therapy still include the massage techniques of the old *anma* using direct points along the meridians. It is believed that shiatsu therapy would not fatigue the muscles like the old style of *anma*.

A History of Shiatsu

Shiatsu can be traced back to India through a Buddhist priest named Bodhidharma, who made a trip to China in 530 B.C. During a visit to the original Shaolin Temple, he noticed the monks had difficulty staying awake during meditation. Discovering they also were in poor physical condition, he introduced a system of exercises for health and sensory control referred to as Tao-Yinn, pronounced as "Do-In."

Bodhidharma's system featured controlled self-massage and self-application of pressure points along the meridians of the body. This system was used to promote detoxification and rejuvenation of the blood flow, thereby creating renewed energy flow throughout the body.

Tao-Yin soon became a major part of the monks' health practices. This method, along with other Chinese healing arts, soon spread to other parts of Asia and the Orient. By the 10th century, many of the Chinese healing arts, including Tao-Yin, were introduced to Japan.

During the Edo era, Japanese doctors were required to study and practice *anma* therapy to familiarize themselves with the energy meridian channels, body functions, body structure, and pressure points. This helped them diagnose and treat illnesses using a variety of cures.

Shiatsu began its modern era in 1920 thanks to Tokujiro Namikoshi, who established the Shiatsu Institute of Therapy in Hokkaido, Japan. Later, Shizuto Masunaga opened his own shiatsu school. Today, there are two major shiatsu methods taught in Japan. Tokujiro Namikoshi's system is characterized by application of pressure to a direct reflex point, which relates to the central and autonomic nervous system. The Shizuto Masunaga, on the other hand, is characterized by sensitivity to the energy channels, which display mind-body function.

Today in the Western world, one can find several derivatives of these two strains of shiatsu stemming from Japan. They include: Zen Shiatsu; Ohashiatsu; Nippon Shiatsu; Acupressure Shiatsu; Five Element Shiatsu; and Macrobiotic Shiatsu.

Shiatsu for Headaches

For purposes of this book, we will be using the chair reversal, so the patient is facing the back of the chair. This exposes the back area on which to be worked. The treatment begins with the patient and therapist breathing together in harmony with their Ki. It is essential for the patient (if need be) to learn some basic breathing techniques. It is also important for the patient to take deep breaths when Shiatsu is applied so the treatment will not cause discomfort or pain. Shihan Benjamin Kahananui shows you the proper technique.

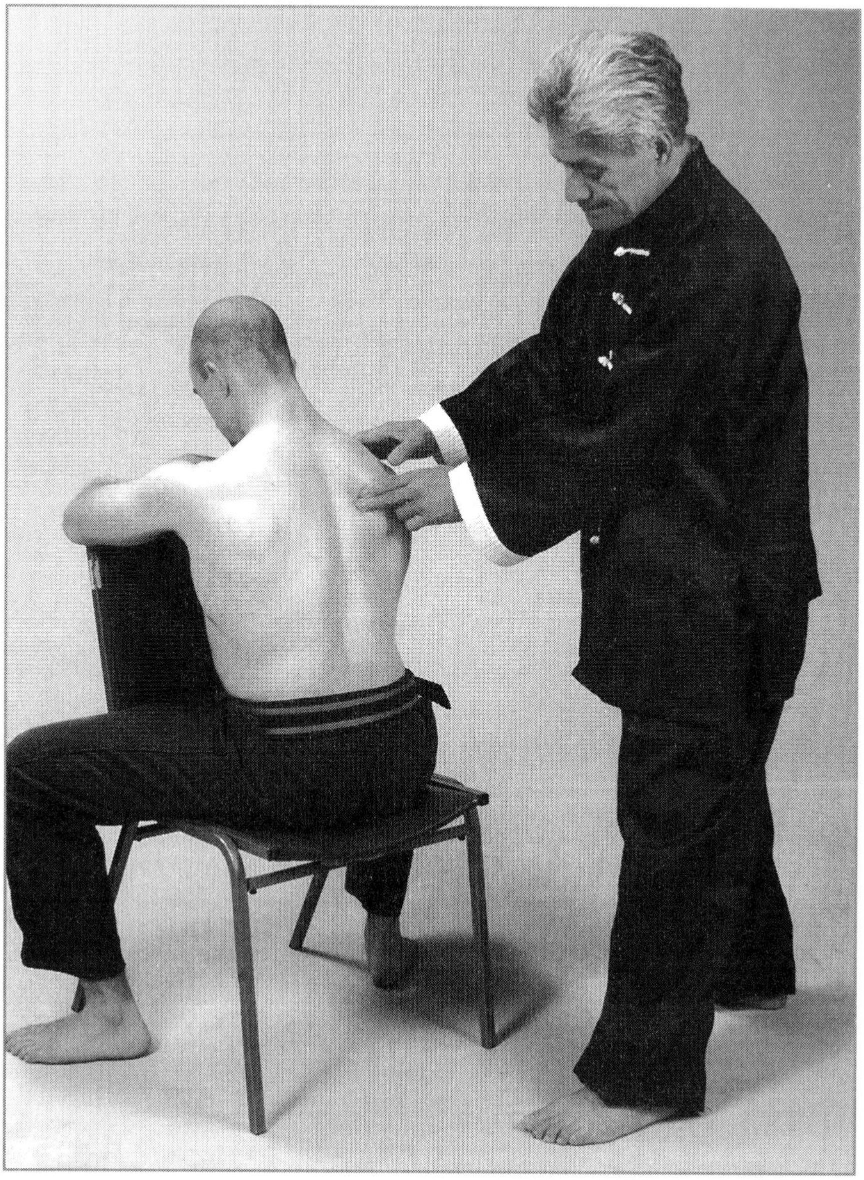

The shoulder blades (scapulae, in front) will be your beginning point as a therapist. There are five points on the inter-scapular area (between the spinal column and scapula) running from the upper to the lower corner of the scapula and parallel with the spinal column. The most important points are #3 (the middle) and #2 (one step up). Apply pressure for three-to-five seconds on each point.

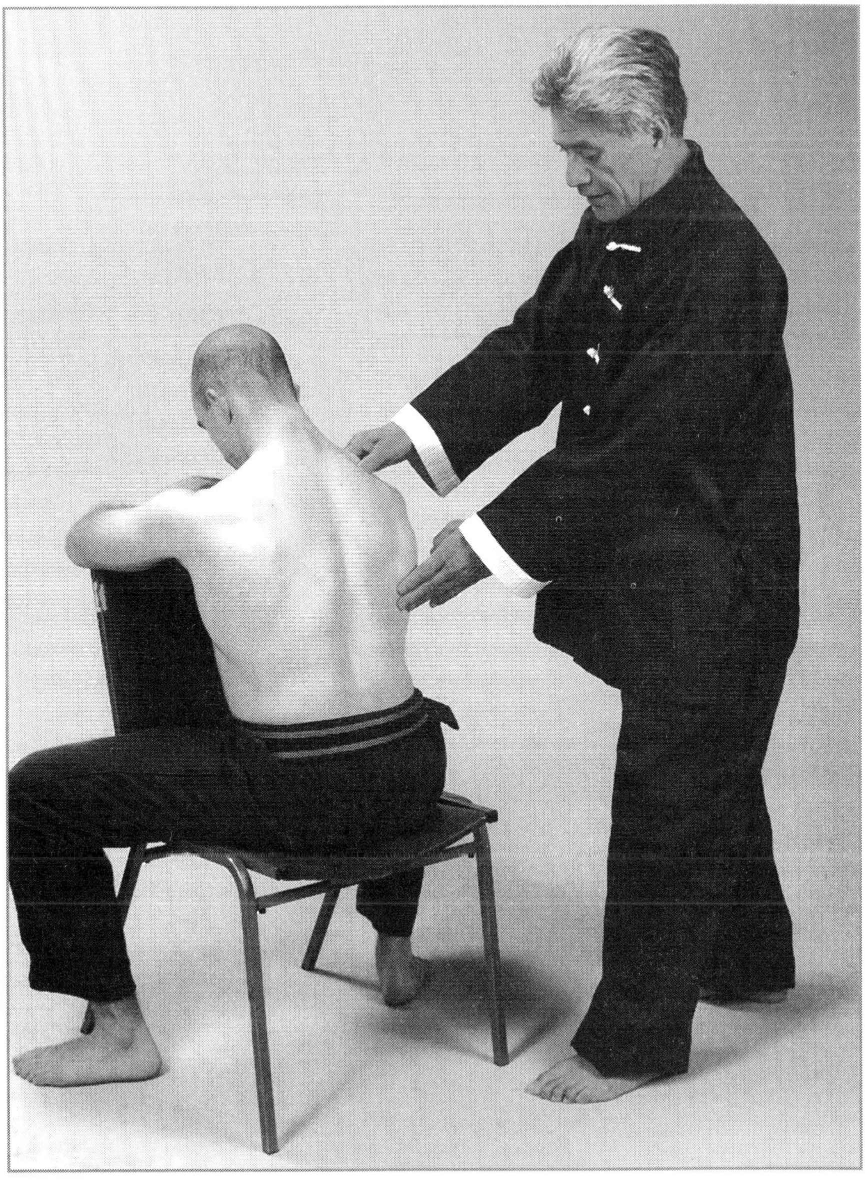

Apply pressure to the #1 point of the inter-scapular. It may be tender, so be gentle until you can work out the pain. Repeat and go over numbers #5-4-3-2-1 in that order four more times.

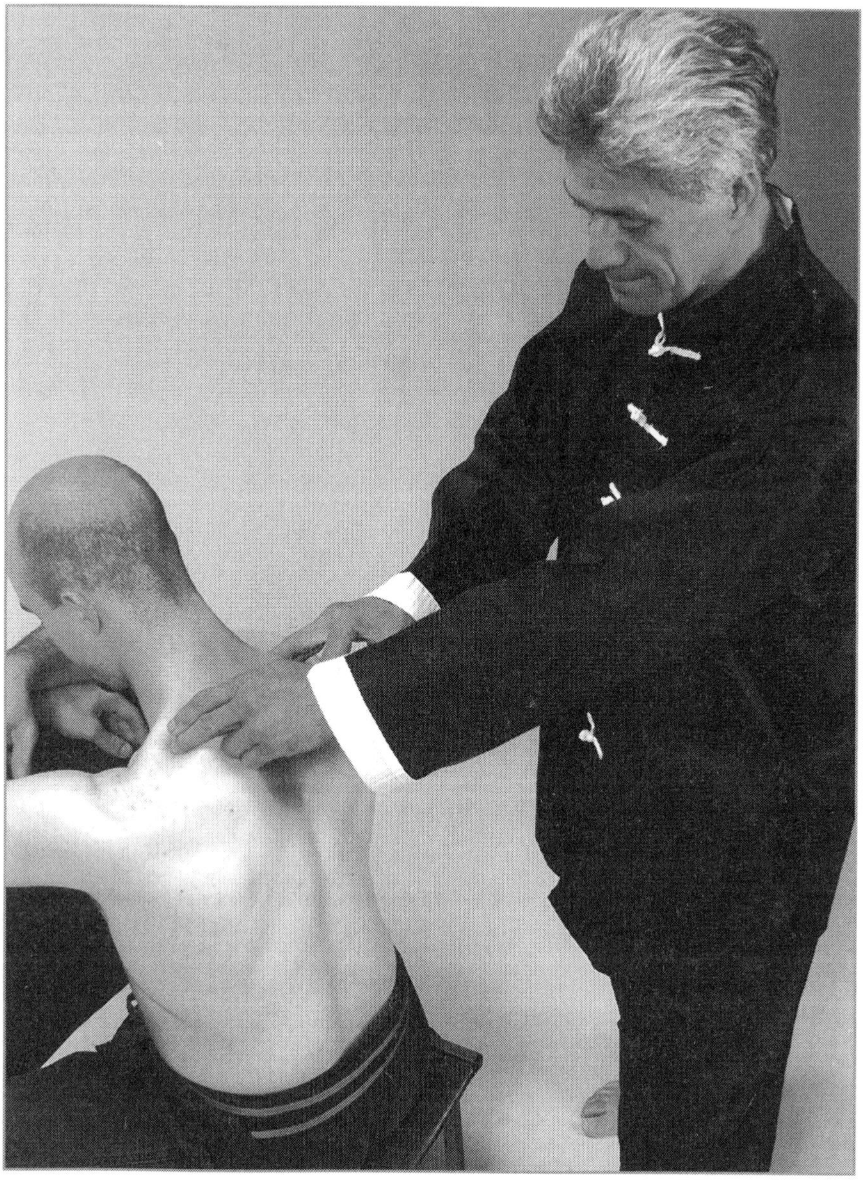

This point is the supra-scapular and may be tender at times. This could require the use of Ki (energy form) to help relax and soothe the cells within the wall lining under this specific point. Remove the pressure to release toxicity from the point and apply pressure again for three-to-five seconds.

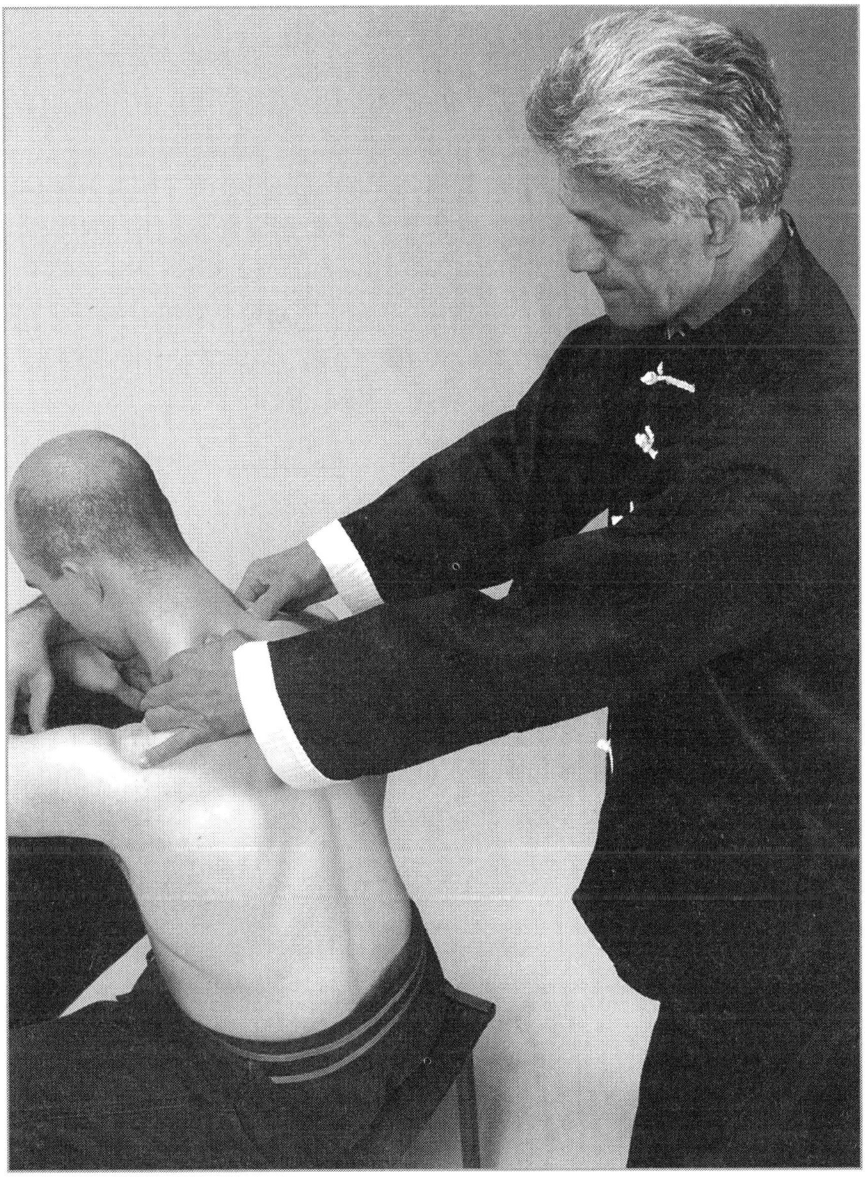

The base of the posterior cervical area consists of four points going up both sides along the cervical vertebrae. The point begins with #4. Apply pressure for three-to-five seconds and move up to #3 and #2.

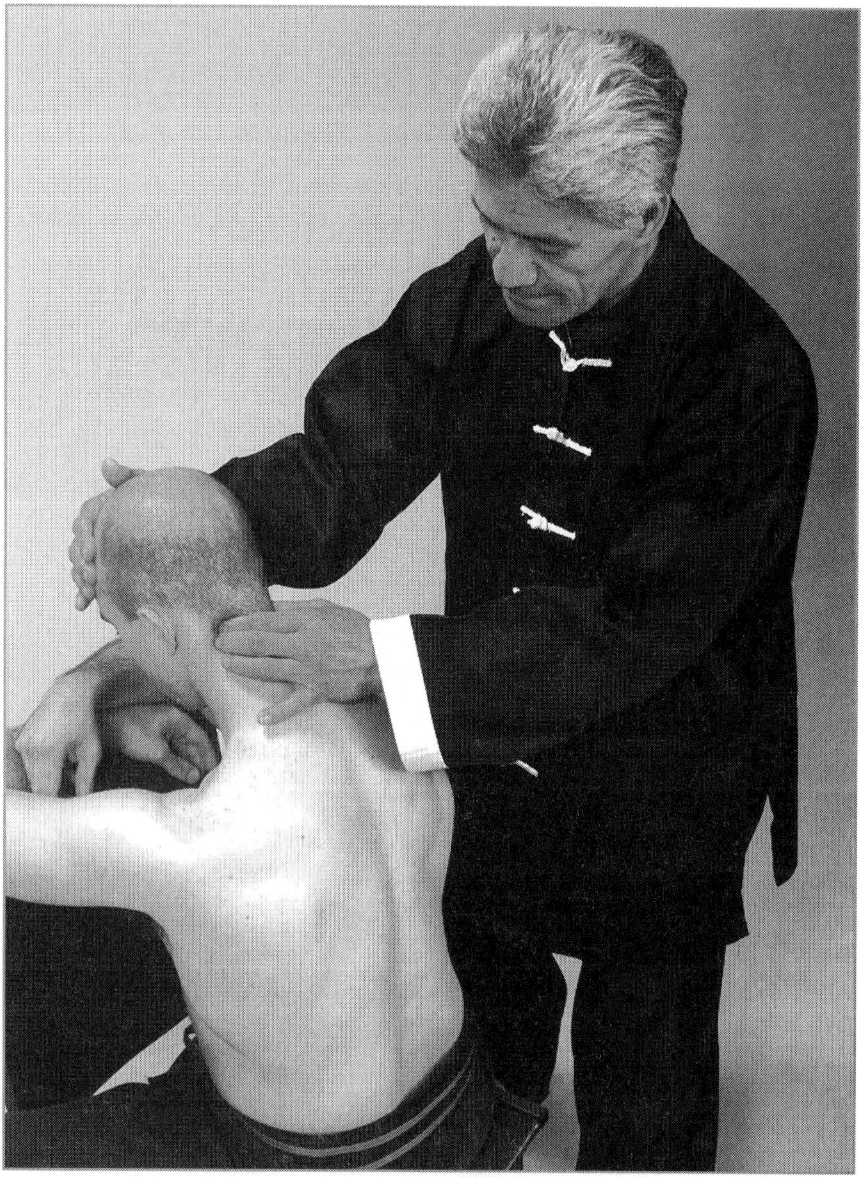

This is the base of the skull area or #1 point where many people get their headaches. Pain is difficult to handle in this area. Breathe deeply and exhale as pressure is applied. Go from #4 through #1, holding for three-to-five seconds, and repeat three times.

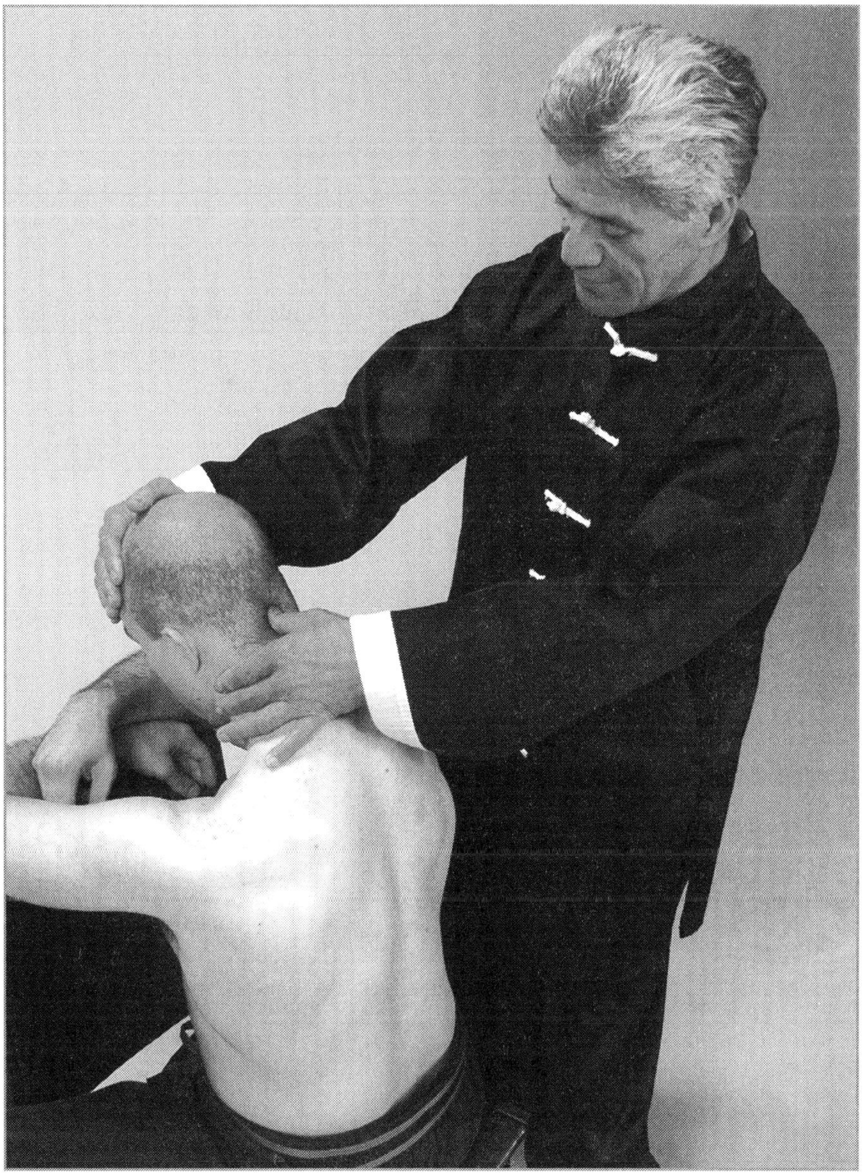

The top center at the base of the skull is a soft spot or point called the Medulla Oblongata. Ki extension can help stabilize energy flow to the brain and head areas.

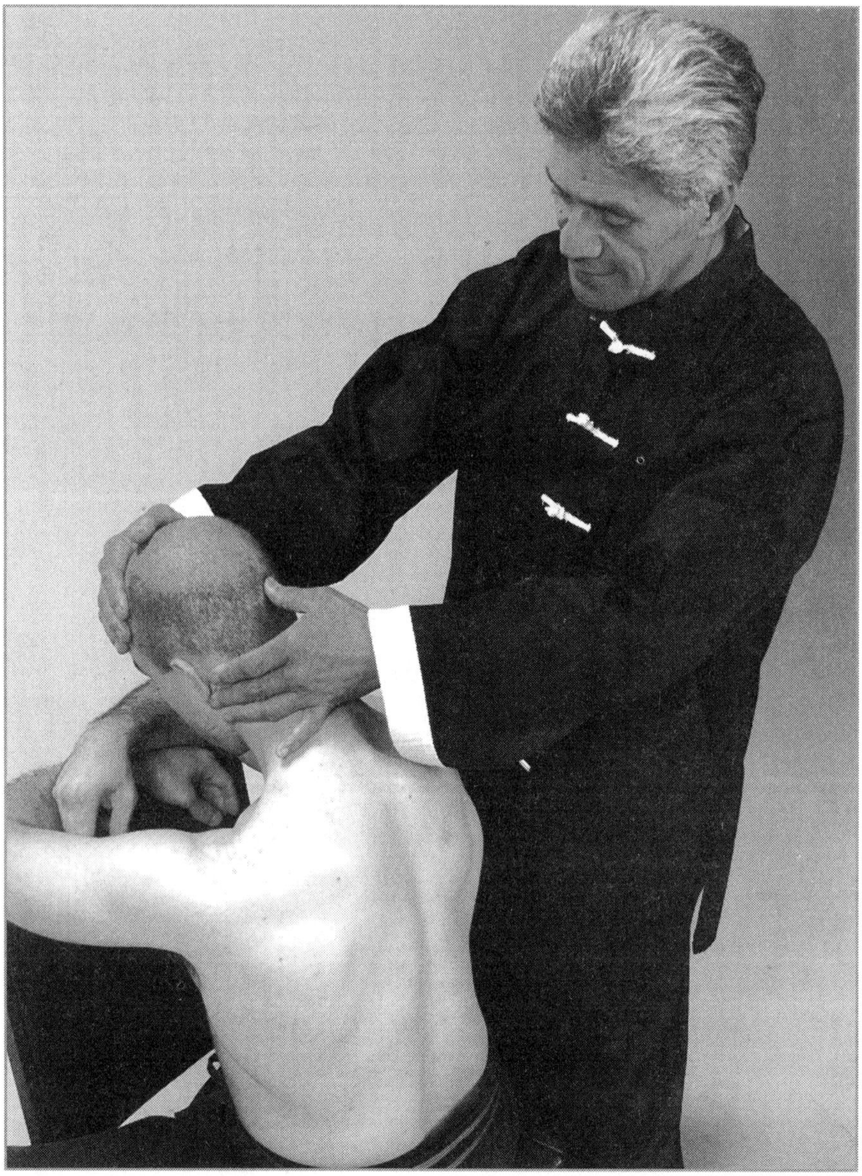

When you move from the Medulla Oblongata along the median line you'll find three points called the Occipital Cervical Region. Apply pressure for three seconds per point and repeat three times.

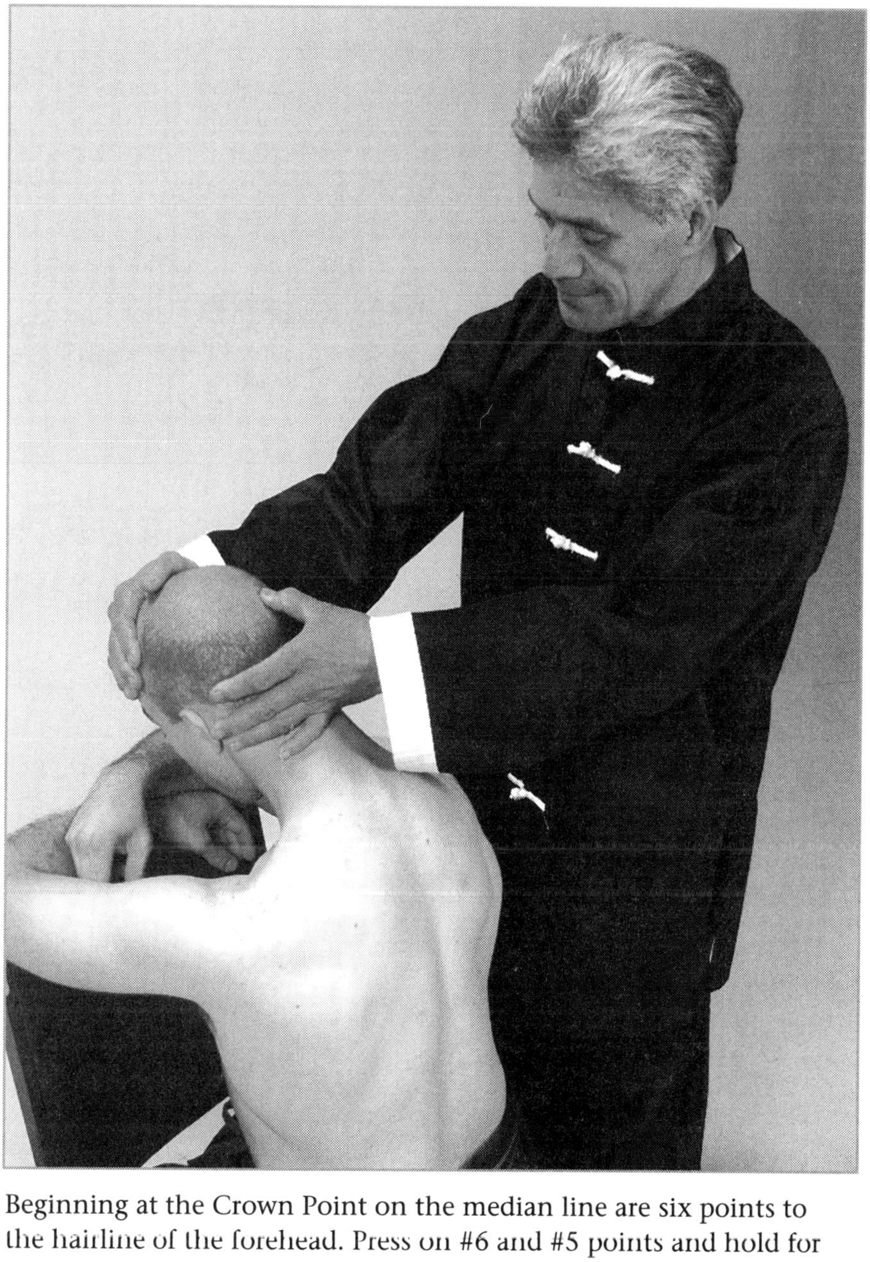

Beginning at the Crown Point on the median line are six points to the hairline of the forehead. Press on #6 and #5 points and hold for three seconds.

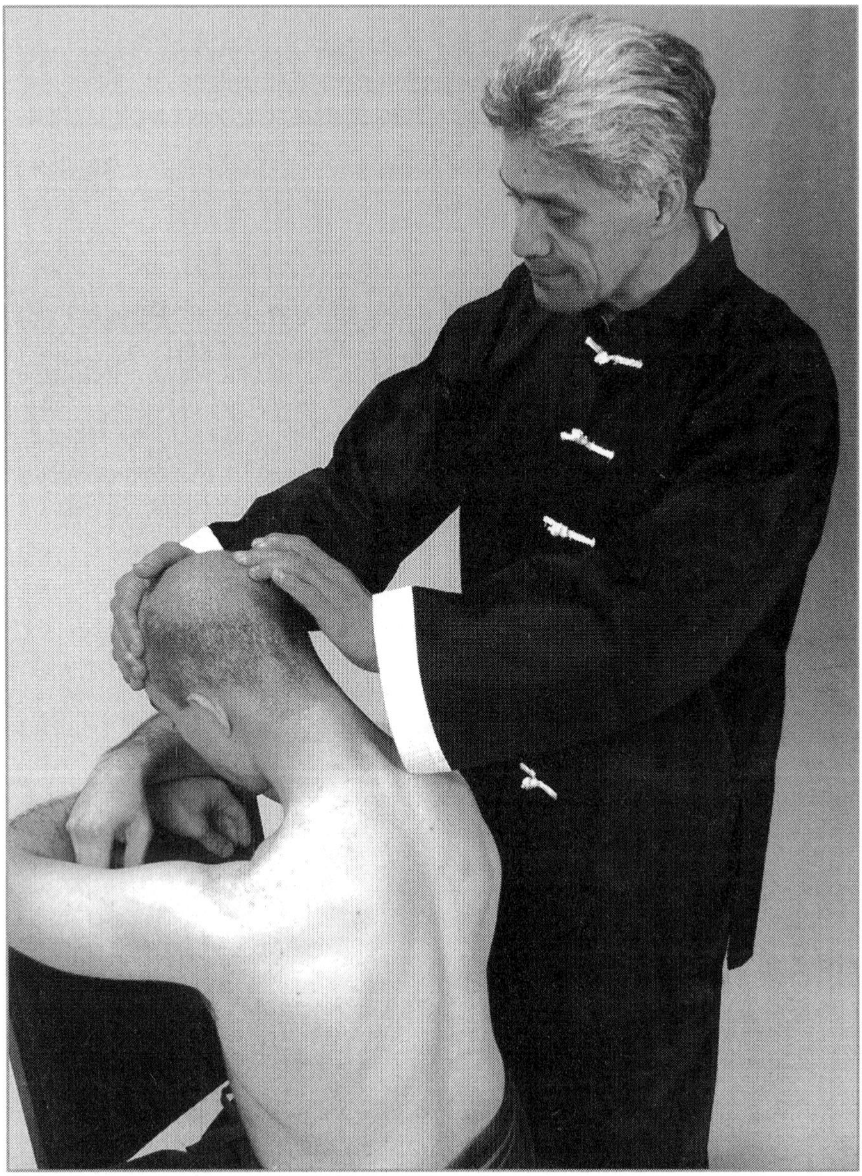

Continue to apply pressure on #4 and #3 point and hold for three seconds.

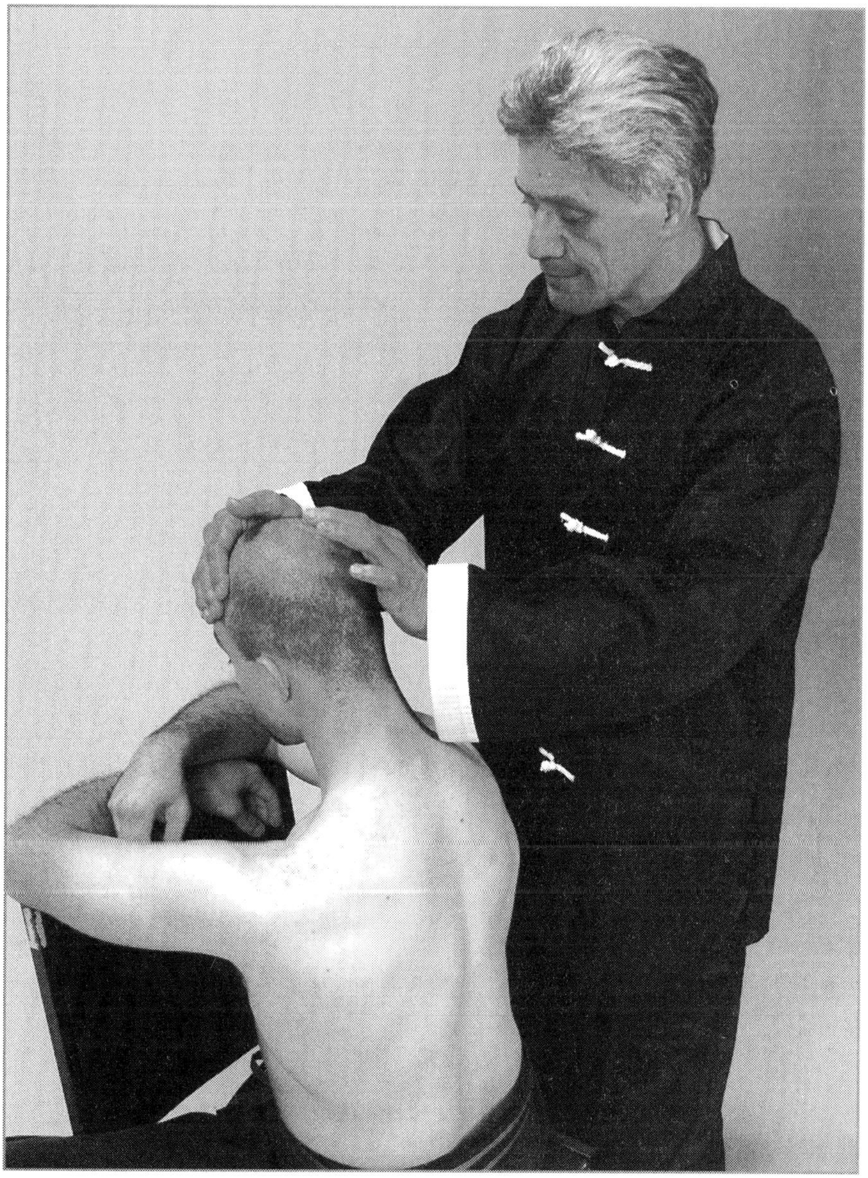

Continue to apply pressure on #2 and #1 points and hold for three seconds. Repeat procedures illustrated in #18 through #20 (points #1 through #6) three times.

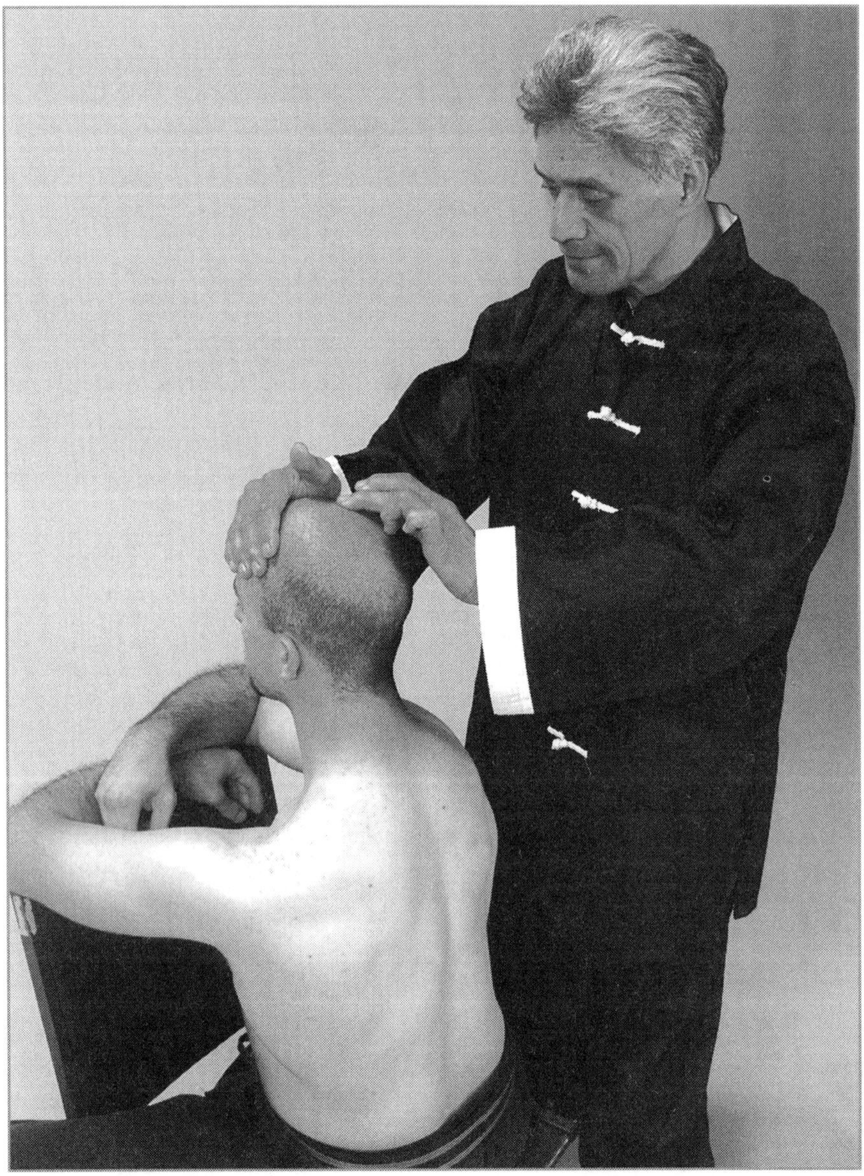

This demonstrates how you can use the index, middle and ring fingers to apply pressure to the right temporal region, which covers 18 points on the right of the meridian line. All points are held for three seconds and repeated three times.

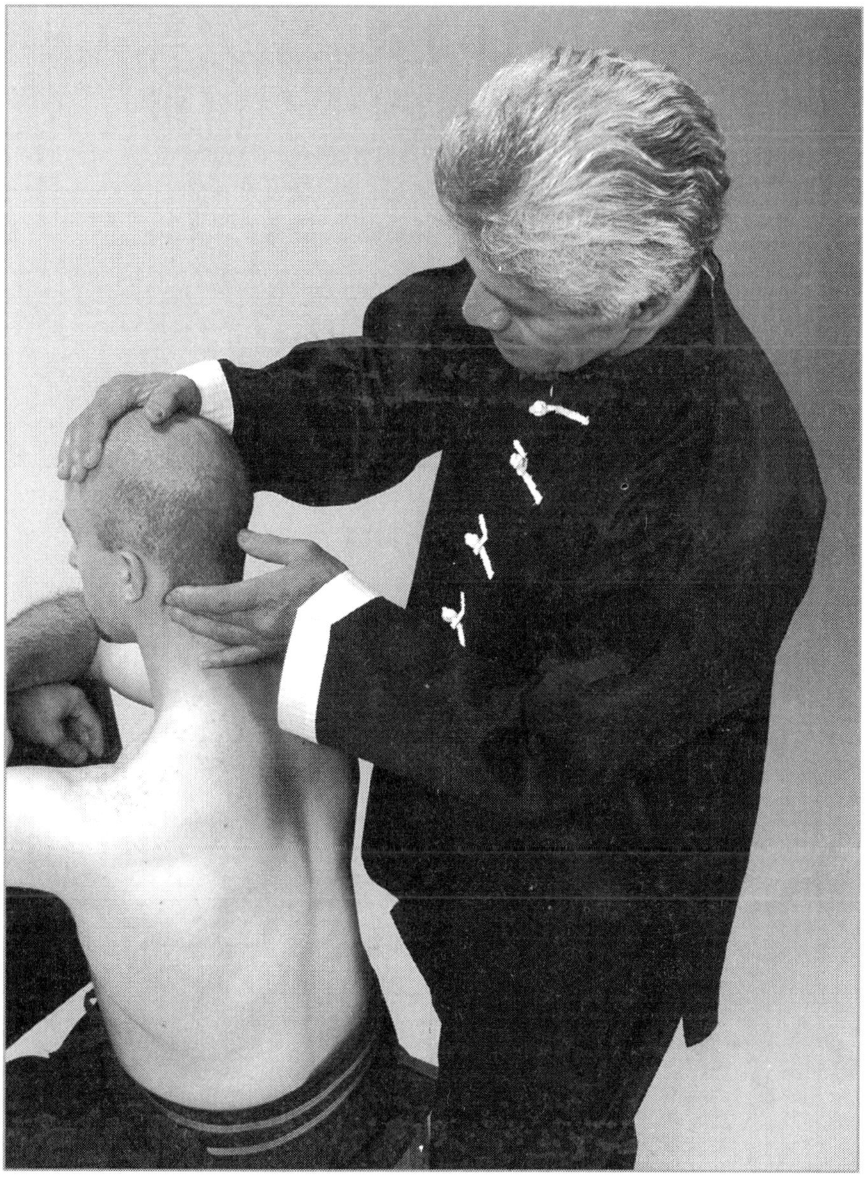

This demonstrates the use of the thumb to apply pressure on the left temporal region pressure points. Although it takes a little longer, expect to see the same results.

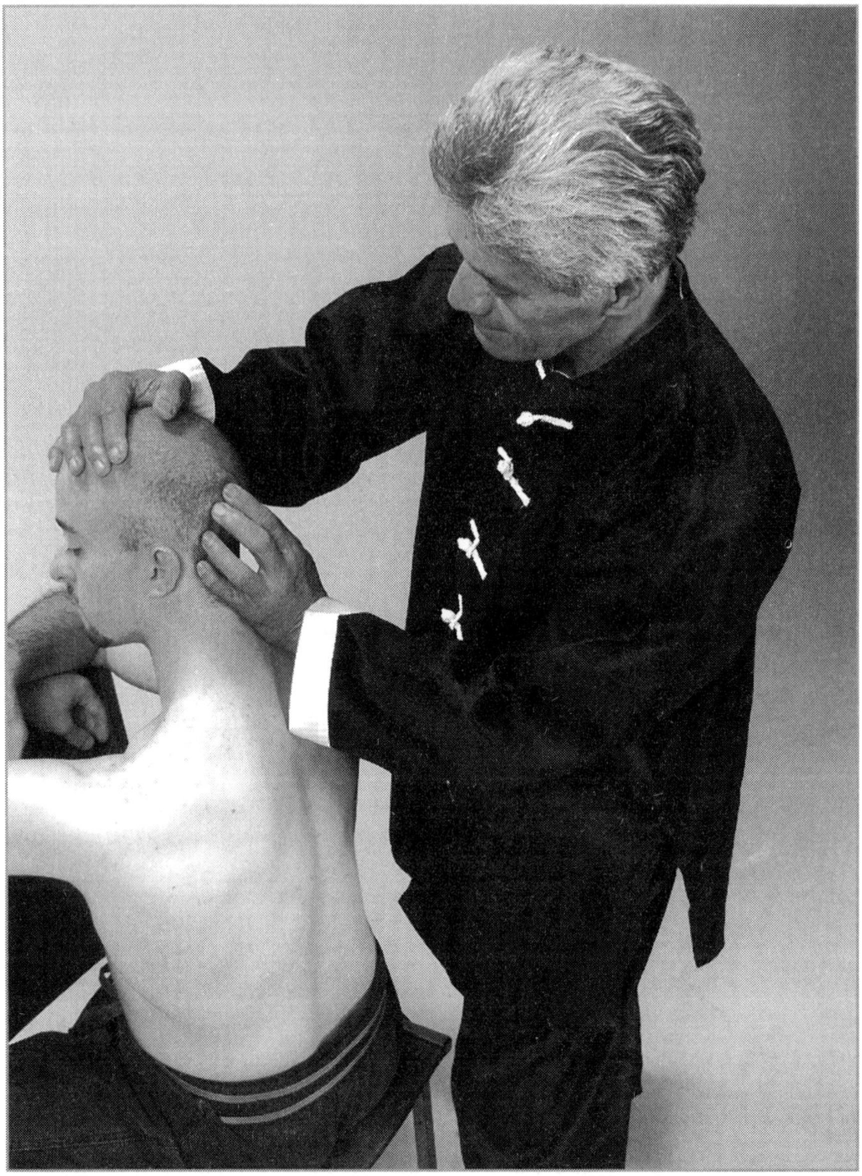

This demonstrates the use of the index, middle and ring finger on the left temporal region covering 18 points. Three points are addressed each time. Hold for three seconds at all points and repeat pressure three times each.

Shiatsu for Lower Back Pain

Note: The ten points in the Medial Femoral area can be added to help relieve lower back pain. Each point should be pressed for five seconds and repeated three times.

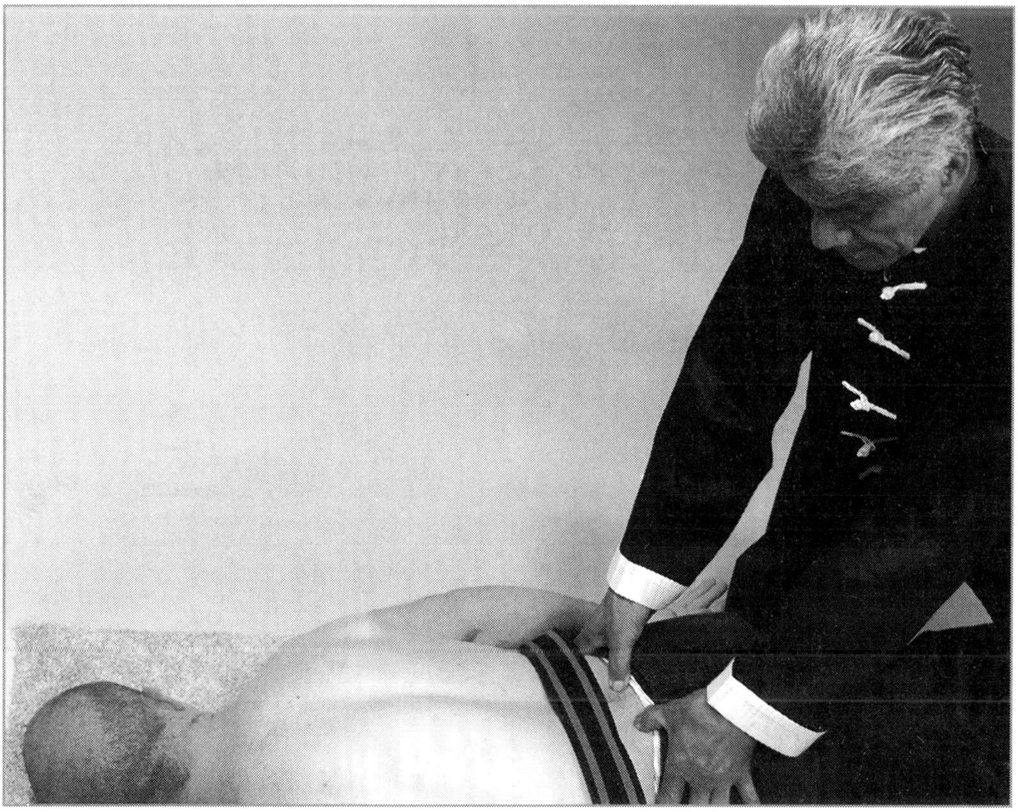

Begin by feeling for possible tenderness near the lower lumbar area. If needed, use Ki (energy force) to relieve the tenderness before applying thumb pressure on point #1 on the Iliac Crest. This is held for five seconds.

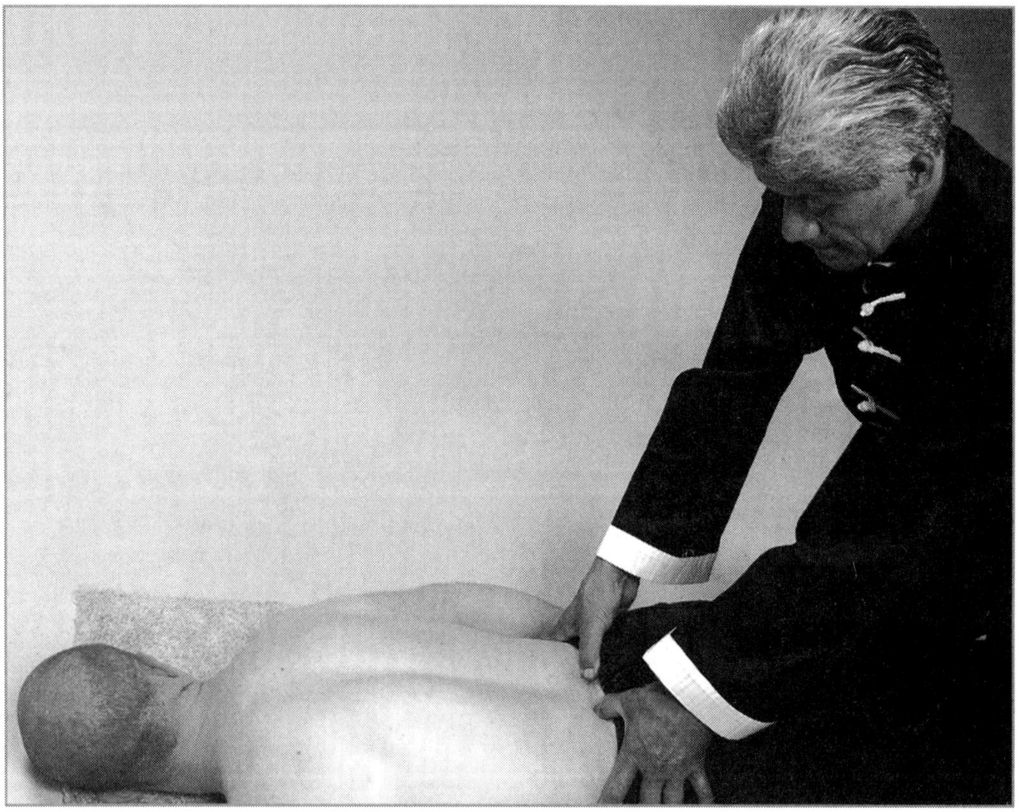

Move outward to point #2, holding the applied pressure for five seconds.

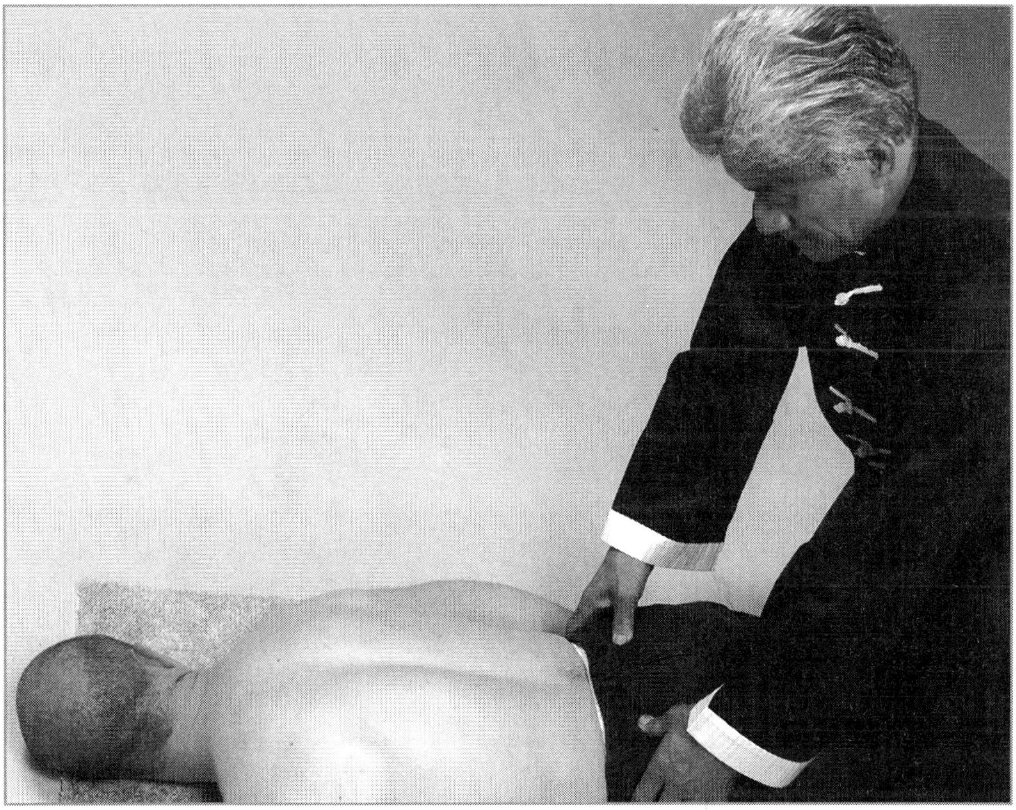

Continue moving to point #3 using the same pressure for five seconds. Repeat steps one and three above, three more times.

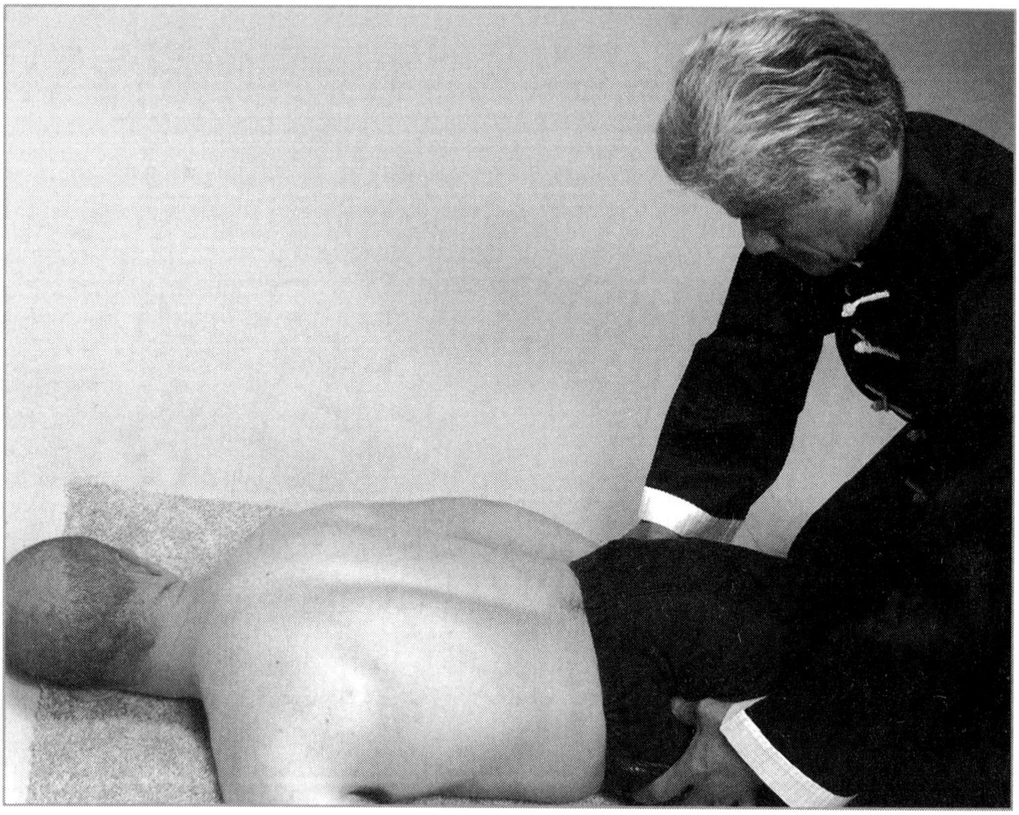

Apply pressure on the Namikoshi point. If tender, use Ki (energy force) to relieve the tenderness before applying pressure.

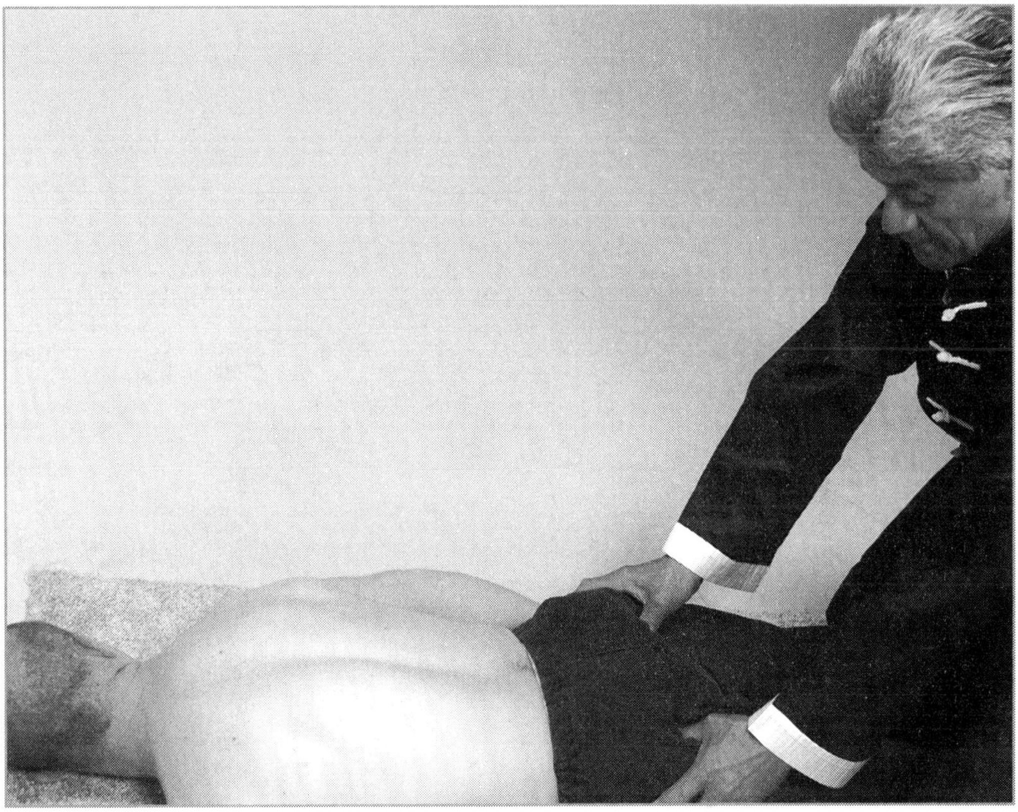

Work the Sacral Area, centerline of the Sacrum, and apply pressure cautiously moving downward in a 45-degree angle to the fourth point of the Glutei Region.

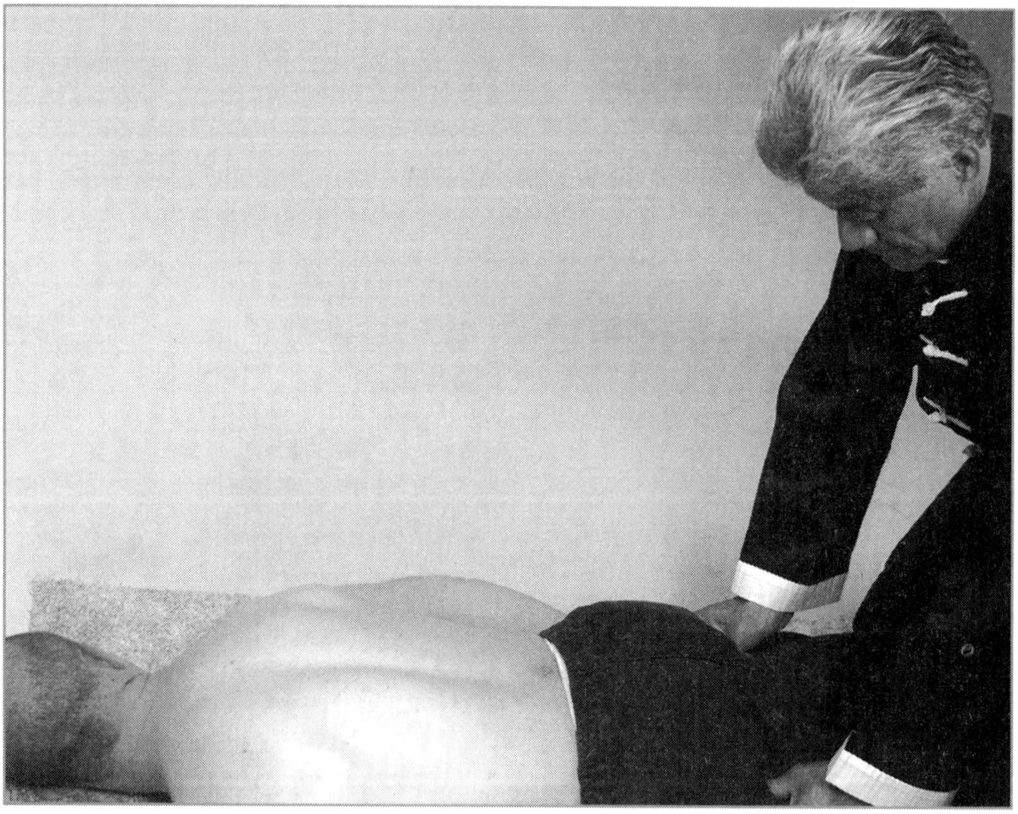

This is point #1 of the Posterior Femoral Area of the Glutei fold. Points #1 through #10 need pressure applied to each and should be held for five seconds. Repeat three times.

Lomi-Lomi

Derived from the same category as the old system of *anma,* lomi-lomi was discovered in the Polynesian Islands, where it can still be found in a few small pockets. Many of the old *kahuna* (witchdoctors) were practitioners of lomi-lomi and some of the techniques are still being passed from generation to generation. Lomi-lomi masters apply a dynamic kneading or rolling method alongside the meridians of the body, followed by a quick release to allow a fresh flow of blood to that area. This blood flow also can be referred to as energy flow. With new blood flow comes new oxygen flow, which helps to begin its natural healing process. Because of its dynamic application, the body goes through a period of fatigue before relaxation.

Because of the Japanese influence in Hawaii, shiatsu is practiced widely throughout the islands. It is used more than any other massage therapeutic program.

Research has shown that a person who sits at a desk eight hours a day may only achieve about 25 percent of his activity capacity in the first two-to-three hours of work. But following a 20-minute shiatsu session every morning, the activity rate rises to nearly 95 percent. Many corporations are experimenting with shiatsu in the workplace, theorizing that an early energy boost leads to greater productivity. In essence, the better employees feel the more refreshed they are. This leads to a better utilization of manpower.

Studies also have shown that the final two hours of an employee's workday are less productive when he has not received a morning shiatsu treatment. However, with the therapy, there is no decrease in effort of productivity. Thus, the generation of more productive manpower is at hand. Shiatsu produces muscles that are alive and invigorated.

Kiatsu

Kiatsu is acupressure using Ki or the mind. Serious concentration is developed through this type of training. This will tremendously enhance the giver's Ki extension and promote healing quicker than if the injured area was allowed to stagnate. Kiatsu is the use of pressure in or around the injured area for a few seconds. Pressure forces stagnant blood from the area and when that pressure is released, new blood is pumped into the injured spot.

The body is programmed to respond to any trauma. Injury to the cells releases chemical messengers into the blood stream. These messengers signal white blood cells to stick to the capillary walls in the area of trauma. These white blood cells migrate through the capillary wall and into the damaged tissue. This migration increases the permeability (leakiness) of the capillary walls, which allows fluid to escape into the injured area. This is what you see as swelling. Additionally, messenger products from the white blood cells, while repairing damaged tissue, cause increased permeability and dilate the capillary wall. The subsequent discoloration from bruising is caused by red blood cells that have come out of the capillaries. As the hemoglobin from the red blood cells is broken down by the white blood cells, the color turns from purple to green to yellow. As more and more white blood cells are recruited to the area, their signals to each other cause increased inflammatory response. This is positive if there is bacteria in the area of the trauma, but in most cases it only adds to the damage in the injured tissue. Kiatsu can help stop the overfilling of the area and the overactivation cascade of white blood cells. This minimizes the initial insult on the body.

Releasing Ki promotes healing faster by introducing new and vigorous blood flow into the area. To start the process, locate the injured area, then mentally picture the area around it. Imagine a line going with the flow of the muscles, not against it. You can use your finger, thumb, or even your elbow (only if you have been practicing Kiatsu for a while). Apply slight pressure at your starting point, which should be approximately two-to-three inches from the injured area, count to seven and release. Now move you finger or thumb down another inch or two and repeat. Continue all the way through and past the injured area. Then, when you have reached the bottom of the injury, start at that point and work your way up, this time going at one-to-two inch intervals about an inch wide. Repeat twice more, each time exerting a little more pressure. Keep going until the receiver insists the pain is too much to bear. By this time you should notice a drastic dissipation in the color and size of the bruise. The receiver should also experience a reduction in pain.

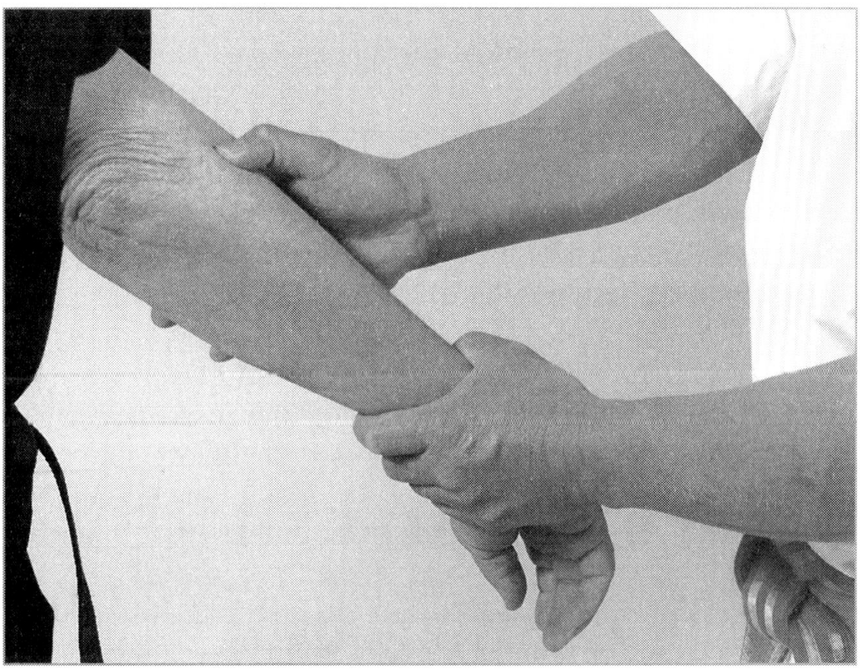

Apply slight finger, thumb, or elbow pressure to a point on and around the injured area. Apply pressure first for a seven-count if the area shows bruising. Move the pressure in increments of one-half-to-one inch, gently massaging along the way. Draw a straight line from the center position of the muscle. Start by going with the grain and applying pressure about three inches past the injured area. Massage one-half-to-one inch again and start over. You can administer slightly harder pressure if the patient is willing.

Oriental Massage

Oriental Massage originated thousands of years ago, mostly in countries such as China, Japan, India, and Korea. It is no coincidence that these countries were among the leaders of the world's first martial arts movement. These massages remain the foundation of virtually every type of massage practiced today. Originally, only family members or close friends were asked to perform massages. In those days, massages were only performed by someone who had great compassion for the other. It was through these attitudes that many of these massage therapies are based.

In China, a method was devised to explain how the changing forces of nature influenced the human body. The *yin* (Earth force) and the *yang* (Heaven's Force) brought a rhythm to the process. For every *yang* there was a *yin,* for every light there was a dark. These unifying opposites brought balance to life. The combination of these two opposites also described the way energy flowed in the body. This system of *yin* soon became the foundation for most Oriental healing.

The Indian health systems believe there are seven gathering areas in the body called *chakras,* which can be found along the central channel of the body. Wherever these heaven and earth forces meet, secondary channels known as meridians (in the Chinese systems) were found. These meridians, the basis for all energy flow in the body, moved away from the central channel, traveled throughout the body and settled in the organs. This energy flow is referred to as Ki and any disruption of Ki will lead to an imbalance that ultimately causes sickness or disease.

Americans have a strong belief in what Eastern medicine refers to as Ki. We believe that there is a balance to all things living—positive-charged protons with a magnetic attraction to negative-charged electrons. This is the theory behind *yin* and *yang*—the movement of charged ions creates a flow of electromagnetic energy (Ki).

The meridians intertwine with each other throughout

the body and assist in providing our energy needs. But the meridians do much more. For example, the kidney meridian also plays a large part in emotions such as fear and courage. If someone pulls a muscle in an area that correlates with the kidney meridian, it may have been an act of fear or courage that originally caused the injury. If you cannot touch the area because of injury, you can probably stimulate an area away from the injury but along the same meridian.

There are five elements associated with the meridians—wood, fire, earth, metal, and water. Knowing these five elements will help you understand the flow of energy to the source of a person's symptomatic pain area. It also reveals the interconnective areas between each element. Some may work in conjunction; some may clash altogether.

The Chakras

The seven *chakras* are located along the body's major energy system or primary channel. These channels provide the body's major sources of energy.

The first *chakra* is located near the groin or bottom of the feet and is referred to as the entrance for the earth's upward force or *yin* energy. It governs our physical nature, including our sexual and procreation attitudes.

The second *chakra* is located at the "one point" or *hara,* which is approximately two finger's width below the navel. This *chakra* governs our balance and is the center of our gravity state. It assists the body in its physical movements. It is also the area that stores great energy; if this area is strong it can energize the rest of the body.

Located at the solar plexus, the third *chakra* area can be found at the tip of our diaphragmatic muscles. It is used to teach us to breathe correctly. This *chakra* governs our desire and hunger for life. It influences our stomach, pancreas, gall bladder, spleen, liver and all their functions.

The fourth *chakra* is located at the sternum and is also referred to as the "heart *chakra.*" This controls our emotions and influences our heart and lungs and its functions. It is considered the mediator between our physical and spiritual being.

The fifth *chakra* is located at the throat area, and governs our ability to communicate with others.

The sixth *chakra* is located at the third eye area. This *chakra* governs our mental stage and determines whether or not we are in balance. It also helps us see into the future.

The seventh *chakra* is located at the crown of the head and serves as the entrance for Heaven's downward energy force or *yang* energy. This *chakra* governs our spiritual understanding. The first and seventh *chakras* are attracted to each other and will seek each other in the primary channels. When they meet, they will express themselves toward the other *chakra* points.

Knowing and understanding the various *chakras* and their development will help us determine an imbalance in one of the main channels. The meeting of heaven and earth's forces stimulate all body functions and organs. Therefore, if one or more *chakra* centers are disturbed, we can locate and work with the appropriate meridian to create balance by stimulating the *chakra* in question.

Chapter 9

Yoga

There are several popular types of Yoga being practiced today, including Hatha, Raja, Karma, and Gnani. What follows is a description of the way I perceive Hatha Yoga. Since I have been a student of Hatha for only a short time, I can only tell you about my brief experience. Yoga has the philosophy, which deals with the physical body: its care, its well-being, its health, its strength, and all that tends to keep it in its natural and normal state.

A *yogi* (male) or a *yogini* (female) practices Yoga to create a balance in which blood and oxygen freely move to all parts of the body. This allows energy to flow to various meridians, which in turns provides you with the best chance of remaining healthy and disease free. Hatha can be traced back to 2,000 B.C. It is said that even Prince Buddha was an avid student of Yoga. According to the newsletter *A Gentle Way Yoga,* by Lanita Varshell:

"Yoga, the oldest science of life, is not only a great form of body conditioning, but [it] can teach you to bring stress under control, not only on a physical level, but on mental and spiritual levels too. The human body can be compared to a car. There are five things that any automobile needs to run properly, whether it is a Rolls-Royce or a rusty old car: lubrication, a cooling system, electric current, fuel, and a sensible driver behind the wheel. In Yoga, the asanas or postures lubricate the body. They keep the muscles and joints running smoothly, tone all the internal organs, and increase circulation without creating fatigue. The body is cooled by complete relaxation while *pranayama* or *yogic* breathing increases *prana,* the electric current. Fuel is provided by food, water and the air you breathe. Lastly, you have meditation, which stills the mind, the driver of the body. By meditating, you learn to control the body, your physical vehicle."

Anyone of any age, condition, or religion can practice. Through training in Hatha Yoga, I have learned that much emphasis is placed on the breathing and the concentration of energy (or Ki) flow to various portions of the body. This is an exciting way to return nature to its original life-force.